MW01258998

Qigong

An Essential Beginner's Guide to Developing Your Chi and Cultivating Healing Energy

Your Free Gift (only available for a limited time)

Thanks for getting this book! If you want to learn more about various spirituality topics, then join Mari Silva's community and get a free guided meditation MP3 for awakening your third eye. This guided meditation mp3 is designed to open and strengthen ones third eye so you can experience a higher state of consciousness. Simply visit the link below the image to get started.

https://spiritualityspot.com/meditation

Contents

Chapter 1: The Art and Benefits of Qigong

The word Qigong comes from two Chinese characters representing the words chi and gong. Chi refers to here, breath, or gas. Often, it's translated into a metaphysical form called vital energy. This energy is intended to circulate throughout the entire body. She can also be generally defined as a universal energy that includes electromagnetic, light, and heat energy. Being the central foundational principle in traditional Chinese medicine and martial arts, various definitions of the word often include breathing, air, and the interactions between spirit, energy, and matter.

Gong, or "Kung," on the other hand, is often interpreted as work. Many people define it as a specific form of practice, accomplishment, result, service, achievement, merit, or mastery. People also use the word to refer to gong fu, also known as Kung Fu, as a way to express effort that leads to accomplishment.

Combining these two words, Qigong describes a particular practice or way of doing things that help promote health and well-being through the cultivation and balancing of life energy.

During the 1940s and 1950s, Qigong was a word used to describe a wide range of Chinese exercises that focused on health and science. People have started to gradually shift their focus away from its original Chinese roots, i.e., the spiritual practices and mysticism.

History of Qigong

Qigong is an ancient Chinese practice that has been around for over 4000 years. Throughout its rich history, many Qigong practices have been developed throughout different societal segments in Chinese culture. These include:

1. Confucianism: moral character development and longevity are the main focus

2. Chinese martial arts: if the objective is to develop excellent fighting abilities

3. Traditional Chinese medicine: the main goal is the cure or prevention of illnesses and ailments

4. Buddhism and Daoism: it uses Qigong as an integrative part of meditation

Today, modern Qigong combines many different traditions. Often, these are diverse or even disparate. A good example of this is combining Daoism's internal alchemy meditative practice with the ancient standing meditation practice of shing chi or circulating chi, the standing meditation practice called Zhan Zhuang, and the Dao Yin breathing exercise called guiding and pulling.

Normally, Qigong masters taught the practice to their students verbally and through actual training. In particular, they emphasized scholarly meditation practices together with dynamic or gymnastic practices used by many people in Chinese society.

But beginning in the late 40s and throughout the 1950s, The Chinese Communist Party government attempted to combine the many different forms of the practice to establish credible scientific bases for Qigong. For example, Liu Guizhen established Qigong as a set of life-enhancing practices better founded on many philosophical traditions such as the Dao Yin. For many experts, this was the start of the modernization of the sanctification of Qigong.

From 1958 to 1963, the period popularly known as the Great Leap Forward, and during The Cultural Revolution from 1966 to 1976, the Communist Party imposed a tight rein over the practice. Along with other Traditional Chinese medical practices, public access to Qigong was severely limited through very tight controls. In government-run rehabilitation centers, the practice was promoted. As a result, Qigong continued to spread throughout China through hospitals and universities. Once the Cultural Revolution ended, Qigong became even more popular as a daily morning exercise practiced by throngs of people throughout the country.

After the death of Mao Zedong, Qigong became even more popular during Deng Xiaoping and Jiang Xiemin's reign from 1976 through much of the 1990s. During this time, anywhere from 60 to 200 million Chinese citizens were performing Qigong throughout the nation. As it became more popular, controversies and problems also started popping up. These include:

> 1. Qigong deviation, which was considered as a mental condition

> 2. Using pseudoscience in establishing Qigong practitioner credibility

> 3. The creation of many cults centered on the practice

> 4. Exaggerated claims of extraordinary capabilities, many of which may be classified as out of this world

> 5. So-called Qigong masters exaggerating their claims to benefit from the practice personally

The Chinese government established the national Chi Gong Science and Research Organization in 1985 to properly regulate the numerous Qigong-related denominations that have sprouted all over the country. The Chinese government finally enforced control measures on the public practice of Qigong in 1999 in reaction to the continued spreading of the practice, which resulted in the massive revival of old Chinese traditions that authorities felt were a threat, such as

1. Morality

2. Spirituality

3. Mysticism

Part of the public control measures implemented on Qigong practitioners includes - closing clinics and hospitals that promoted the practice as part of their healing protocols and banning groups that promote the same such as Falun gong. Ever since the implementation of crackdowns, The Chinese government has only supported the research and practice of Qigong as part of traditional Chinese medicine. Any context related to spirituality and other non-health and medical contexts continues to be rejected.

In line with this approach, The Chinese Communist Party or CCP created the Chinese Health Qigong Association in 2000. This regulatory body tightly controls the public practice of Qigong by:

1. Limiting Qigong related public gatherings

2. Requiring instructors to be trained and certified by the government

3. Restricting Qigong practices to those that the government approves

Despite strict government measures, Qigong managed to spread worldwide because of three factors; The Chinese diaspora, globalization, and the rapid growth of the tourism industry in China. As a result, billions of people regularly practice Qigong, believing in its many benefits. Just like how it started, global citizens who have adopted Qigong as part of their lifestyle come in a wide range of nationalities and races. They do so for a myriad number of reasons, which include:

1. Recreation

2. Physical fitness

3. Preventive health

4. Alleviation of sicknesses and many medical conditions

5. Martial arts training

6. Spiritual growth

7. Meditation

General Qigong Practices

Based on ancient Chinese philosophy, Qigong covers a wide range of practices that aim to develop excellent coordination between a person's body, mind, and breath. These include meditation (both still and moving), chanting, massage, non-contact treatments, and sound meditation. All of these are performed using a wide variety of body postures.

Typically, Qigong can be classified into two main categories: active or dynamic Qigong and passive or meditative Qigong. Active Qigong, also known as Dong gong, is performed with slow but flowing movements. But passive Qigong (jing gong) is done by focusing on the inner movement of the breath and being in a still position.

When performed as a moving type of meditation, Qigong involves slow movements, mental focus, and deep diaphragmatic breathing. While doing this, you will be seeing chi flowing through your body in your mind's eye.

When doing this type of Qigong, your movements need to be fluid, often carefully choreographed, and must be synchronized with your breathing and awareness. Many of the best examples of these types of movements can be found in the following Chinese practices:

1. Tai Chi

2. Baguazhang

3. Xing Yi Quan

4. Wu Qin Xi Qigong, also known as The Five Animals Movements

As a kind of gentle physical exercise, you'll perform repeated movements that can help strengthen and stretch your body, increase fluid circulation in your body, improve proprioception and balance, and improve your awareness of how you move through space.

Passive Qigong

When you perform passive Qigong, you must hold certain postures for extended periods of time. To an extent, static Qigong resembles yoga. Examples of static postures are the Chinese martial art called Yiquan, which is based on Xingyiquan that puts a premium on static stance exercises. Another good example is the eight pieces of brocade or Baduanjin Qigong. This particular form of healing also involves a series of static postures.

You may also perform passive Qigong through breathing meditation, which uses breathing awareness, mantras, visualization, sounds, chants, and emphasis on Chinese philosophical concepts like moral values, aesthetics, and qi circulation. Meditative Qigong practices are used in a variety of ways. These include:

1. Balancing of qi flow throughout the body's pathways, including the meridian and cultivation of chi in the body's Dantian energy centers, As used in Taoist and traditional Chinese medical practices

2. Stilling the mind via outward focus an object or place or through internal focus using a mantra, emptiness, the breath, or a koan as part of Buddhist traditions

3. Self-enlightenment by focusing on virtues and humanity, as used in Confucian scholar traditions

Using Outside Objects

You may also practice Qigong using external objects such as eating herbs, getting a massage, interacting with other living things, and physical manipulation. In Daoist practice, for example, you may consume customized drinks and food for medical purposes. With martial arts, you can use body manipulation and massage as a way of using Qigong. You may also benefit from interactions with a Qigong professional specializing in transmitting healing Qigong to other people.

Internal Vs. External

Qigong can also be classified into two different systems from a health and therapy perspective: internal and external. Internal Qigong primarily focuses on self-cultivation and care, while external Qigong involves a professional therapist that transmits or directs Qi to the person, similar to reiki.

Qigong Forms

There are up to 75 forms of Qigong in ancient Chinese literature, while there are up to 56 contemporary forms you can find in a Qigong compendium, many of which were developed by people who have experienced healing through the practice. Generally, all these forms may be classified into five categories:

1. Medical

2. Martial Arts

3. Spiritual

4. Intellectual

5. Life Nourishment

Regardless of if you practice Qigong for health, exercise, or any other reason, it will involve most, if not all, of the following: intentional movement, rhythmic breathing, awareness, visualization, and sound (chanting). Other important aspects of effective Qigong practice include softness of the face (stoic expression), a solid stance (straight spine and firm footing), relaxed muscles and slightly bent joints, and balance/counterbalance of motion over your center of gravity. Some key objectives you'll focus on every session include equanimity, tranquility, and stillness. At the most advanced level, you'll hardly need to move while practicing Qigong.

The Three Qigong Treasures

If you reflect on your life so far, you'll likely remember experiencing a wide variety of emotions. There were times you probably felt euphoric, like you're on top of the world, while in other times, you may have felt like your entire world has crumbled and felt hopeless. You felt such emotions according to your internal state.

When you regularly practice Qigong, you'll be able to achieve optimal physical state through stabilizing your internal resources and life energy replenishment. The process by which you can achieve this is called energy healing.

Speaking of internal resources, practicing Qigong requires three specific ones: jing (essence), qi (energy), and shen (spirit). Called the three treasures of Qigong, these three terms form the key physiological functions of any living being. Therefore, these are crucial for sustaining life.

Qi

This refers to the energy that activates and mobilizes all of our body's structures and procedures. You get qi from various external sources, mostly the food and drinks you consume, the air you breathe, and your surrounding environment. The blood flowing through your veins is led by qi.

Experts consider it the halfway point of the other treasures, i.e., the gate through which passage to and from the body and spirit is possible. Essential for emotional balance and optimum physical health, a strong qi is evident in the ability to express oneself creatively and boldly.

Jing

Jing is qi in stored form, just like body fat is stockpiled. This is the equivalent of calories in the body that are kept for future use. As such, jing is the densest kind of energy among the three and is the one that's most important to your physical body. When you need energy, your body can draw from stored jing and transport it through your body's multiple energy channels. It is the foundation for your body's maturation, growth, and development over time.

Shen

As the final treasure, this resource or energy pertains to your ability to be self-aware and cognizant. Shen is linked closely to your spirit's energy and your behavior and mental health. Many Chinese medical experts have observed that people can lift or brighten their spirits through proper knowledge of their health.

What are the signs that your shen may be dull? These include:

1. Feeling anxious

2. Depression

3. Lethargy

4. Speaking voice that is soft or weak

5. Slurred speech

6. Inappropriate or weird behavior

These symptoms start to appear or become very apparent when the two other treasures can't provide adequate support.

On the other hand, you can tell that your shen is bright when the following are evident:

1. Eyes that are clear and alert

2. Coherent thoughts

3. A deep sense of joy and contentment

4. Speaking confidently and fluently

The Connection Between Your Purpose and the Three Treasures

As their collective name suggests, these three internal resources are crucial for your physical, emotional, and mental well-being, and as such, you must guard them and take care of them very carefully like you would physical treasures. Essentially, these three comprise who you are as a person and help you answer three important life questions:

1. Who are you?

2. Why are you here?

3. What do you want?

Your answers to these three questions are closely linked, much like how intimately related the three treasures are inside your own body.

Daily living eventually leads to weaker connections between your body, spirit, and mind. The greater the disconnections are, the more disconnected you'll feel from your life's purpose. When this becomes chronic, you eventually feel low in energy, lethargic, and unmotivated. Most of the time, your mind's thoughts aren't aligned with your spiritual path. It's pretty much like how you develop unhealthy habits despite knowing they're bad for you. That's why self-defeating or self-destructive actions may be indicative of the disintegration of your qi, jing, and shen.

Qigong's Interaction With Your Three Treasures

Regularly practicing Qigong can help you experience several benefits. The most important one is stabilizing your body, mind, and spirit. For you to experience optimal health and vitality, balance in all areas of your life is crucial. The more you're able to achieve this, the more vitality and harmony you'll experience in your life. On the other hand, you're likely to experience emotional turmoil and physical sickness when you live a chronically imbalanced life.

By regularly practicing Qigong, you'll be able to utilize the three treasures and live a harmonious and aligned life. This is because the practice allows you to integrate your qi, jing, and shen, which helps you achieve greater balance in all key areas of your life, particularly your mind, body, and spirit. When this happens, you'll be able to access your true purpose's highest expression.

Qigong starts to work in your life by helping you become more and more aware of all aspects of yourself, which allows you to gain a deep understanding of who you are. When you're able to do this, you can start strengthening your qi, optimize your jing levels, and ultimately, maximize your shen.

Uses of Qigong

You don't have to be a highly spiritual person, e.g., a monk, to practice Qigong. Like millions of people the world over engage in the practice for many reasons, so can you. A few of the most popular uses of Qigong include:

1. Cultivation of self

2. Exercise

3. Healing

4. Martial arts training

5. Meditation

6. Prevention of sickness is

7. Recreation

8. Relaxation

More than just a variety of uses, people from all walks of life can practice Qigong. From professional athletes to people with physical disabilities, Qigong is a popular form of activity because of its no-impact nature. It can be practiced in various positions, from lying down to standing up. This makes it a very practical form of physical exercise for a wide range of people with physical limitations, such as those recovering from injuries, dealing with disabilities, and are those who are older.

One of the most important uses of Qigong involves traditional Chinese medicine. Its practitioners, and those of integrative medicine and other forms of health practices, consider it a standard medical technique, and they frequently prescribe it for treatment of a myriad number of medical conditions such as

1. Back and leg discomfort

2. Cervical spondylosis

3. Chronic fatigue syndrome

4. Chronic liver conditions

5. Coronary artery disease

6. Diabetes

7. Hypertension

8. Insomnia

9. Menopause

10. Myopia

11. Obesity

12. Stomach ulcers

13. Tumors and cancers

And it's not just traditional Chinese medicine professionals that use Qigong for therapeutic purposes. Outside the U.S., many integrative medical practitioners use it to either supplement established scientific medical treatments. Several of its applications include promoting relaxation, developing fitness, rehabilitation of patients, and treating chronic conditions.

The reported efficacy of Qigong as a form of therapy may only be considered anecdotal. Clinical studies and systematic reviews reveal inadequate evidence for Qigong's efficacy as a medical treatment for specific conditions. It doesn't hurt to try to use it for such purposes. It's because Qigong is generally safe, with no adverse side effects observed during clinical trials across a diverse range of populations. Thus, its reputation as a safe medical practice.

Another reason why using Qigong for therapeutic purposes is its practicality. Using it for self-care and tails very minimal or no cost at all, and when administered as part of group care, its cost efficiency becomes even more glaring.

Qigong isn't completely risk-free. It has its share of associated cautions, too, even if minor or minimal. Things you'll need to exercise caution with as you start to get into it include possible sprains or muscle strains. You can minimize or completely avoid these by making a habit of stretching before Qigong. To minimize or eliminate any potential medical risks, you should first consult with your doctor before starting the practice.

Benefits of the Practice

Throughout the centuries, its practitioners have vouched for and the many benefits they experienced because of regular Qigong practice. These benefits can be generally classified as physiological and psychological.

Physiological Benefits

One of the key physiological benefits associated with the practice is higher bone density. Normally, this benefit is associated with exercises that involve lifting weights or working against resistance. Exercises that involve little or no resistance or weights can have the same effect.

In a 2006 study, researchers discovered that women who regularly perform Qigong for exercise experienced a significant increase in bone mineral density compared to those in a no-exercise control group. Considering that Qigong involves minimal or no resistance or weights, it was a pleasant surprise to find it can help increase bone density.

Another key physiological benefit of performing Qigong regularly is better pulmonary and cardiovascular function. This has been reported in studies like Qigong for Hypertension: A Systematic Review of Randomized Clinical Trials (*Myeong Soo Lee[i], Max H Pittler, Ruoling Guo, Edzard Ernst,* 2007), where subjects' blood pressures went down. The practice also shows potential in lowering heart rate and increasing its variability, both of which are very important health indicators.

You may also develop significantly better body balance when you regularly perform Qigong. One study found that patients who suffer from muscular dystrophy, healthy senior citizens, and women who live sedentary lifestyles improved their balance using Qigong.

To further strengthen your immune system, regularly practicing Qigong may also greatly benefit you. You see, studies have associated Qigong with several positive immune system responses. One of them is a 2004-published clinical trial entitled Assessment of Immunological Parameters Following a Qigong Training Program (*Juan M Manzaneque[i], Francisca M Vera, Enrique F Maldonado, Gabriel Carranque, Victor M Cubero, Miguel Morell, Maria J Blanca*). In the trial, researchers noted that subjects' multiple immune system blood markers improved significantly after one month of Qigong practice compared to just receiving their usual care. One such response is increased antibody levels after getting flu vaccinations for Qigong practitioners compared to those who aren't. Another observed response is significantly better regulation of the inflammation marker interleukin-6 in subjects that regularly practiced Qigong compared to those who didn't.

Finally, regularly practicing Qigong may improve somatic symptoms, which has been shown in various studies like Group and Home-Based Tai Chi in Elderly Subjects With Knee Osteoarthritis: A Randomized Controlled Trial (Brismee J-M, Paige RL, Chyu M-C, Boatright JD, Hagar JM, McCaleb JA, et al.) that was published in 2007. Somatic symptoms include physical discomforts such as pain, shortness of breath, and abdominal discomfort.

Psychological Benefits

It's not just your body that may benefit from this practice, but your mind and emotions too. One of Qigong's best psychological benefits is better life quality, which we can define as your perceived physical health, core beliefs, mental state, relationship with your environment, and social relationships. Several studies – such as the 2007-published study of Lee Y. K. Lee & Woo involving 139 residents of a health care facility - have shown that Qigong can help improve a person's quality of life compared to people who don't practice it.

You may also benefit from better self-efficacy if you practice Qigong regularly. We may define self-efficacy as your confidence in accomplishing things and overcome challenges. Studies like Impact of Qigong Exercise on Self-Efficacy and Other Cognitive Perceptual Variables in Patients with Essential Hypertension (Lee, Myung-Suk & Lim, Hyun-Ja & Lee, Myeong Soo. (2004) had shown that subjects who regularly performed Qigong experienced greater self-efficacy than their inactive control peers, particularly with their received ability to handle challenging or stressful situations.

Regularly performing chi gong may also lower your stress biomarkers or hormones like cortisol, epinephrine, and norepinephrine. Studies such as The Effects of Qigong on Reducing Stress and Anxiety and Enhancing Body–Mind Well-being by Yvonne WY Chow and Andrew MH Siu (2011) have shown lower levels of these stress hormones in subjects that regularly practiced Qigong compared to those that didn't.

Performing this regularly can help you minimize or reduce anxiety and depression if you are suffering from these. Based on depression scales utilized in several studies like the 2005-published randomized control trial (Randomized Controlled Trial of Qigong) in the Treatment of Mild Essential Hypertension (Cheung, Lo, Fong, Chan, Wong, Wong, Lam, Lau, and Karlberg (2005), Qigong helped decrease symptoms of depression in subjects who practiced it compared to those who didn't. Not only that, but it also appears that subjects who do Qigong regularly registered significantly lower anxiety levels compared to an active exercise group. Measurements were taken using the Self-Rating Anxiety Scale.

Scientific Studies on Qigong's Benefits

Compared to Tai chi, Qigong doesn't have as many high-quality research studies to conclusively support many of its reported benefits, most of which are anecdotal. To establish the practice has numerous benefits, more such research studies are needed.

But despite this, Qigong is still worth giving a shot. After all, it's a very safe practice that normally involves relaxation and very gentle movements, both of which are considered good for health in general. Also, practicing Qigong doesn't require spending money. Getting into it gives you opportunities to gain lots of benefits with minimal or no risk.

Still, several studies have documented Qigong-related benefits. One of them was a 2010 published study in the prestigious American Journal of Health Promotion, which reviewed 66 studies involving 6400 subjects. In A Comprehensive Review of Health Benefits of

Qigong and Tai Chi, researchers Roger Jahnke, Linda K Larkey, Carol Elizabeth Rogers, and Jennifer Etnier found various positive results while combing through the studies. Specifically, they found that regular practice of Qigong and Tai chi helped improve the subjects' balance and bone health.

Another important study on Qigong's health benefits was Qigong for Hypertension: A Systematic Review of Randomized Clinical Trials by Myeong Soo Lee, Max H Pittler, Ruoling Guo, and Edzard Ernst. Published in the Journal of Hypertension in 2007, the researchers reported that regular Qigong exercise appeared to improve the subjects' blood pressures mildly, but the study's authors qualified that more study needs to be done to confirm their reported results.

Another study conducted in the same year, published in the Journal of Alternative and Complementary Medicine this time, reported another positive health benefit among its subjects: mild positive effects in diabetes control. In A Qualitative Review of the Role of *Qigong* in the Management of Diabetes (Liu Xin, Yvette D. Miller, and Wendy J. Brown), the authors also issued a similar statement, i.e., more conclusive studies are needed to validate the benefits they reported.

To date, researchers continue to conduct studies on the health benefits of regular Qigong practice. These include the possibility of using Qigong as a complementary cancer treatment.

Chapter 2: Understanding Energy: Qi, Yin-Yang, Jing, and Shen

Qi may be defined as the energy the flows throughout our bodies, which provides us with the necessary minerals, nutrients, and circulation for holistic health. In traditional Chinese medicine, qi is believed to be a person's life force, and as such, it is the best way to gauge vitality.

As an ancient practice, Qigong has been used by doctors who specialize in holistic or integrative medicine and acupuncturists to help their patients restore their bodies to their natural and optimally healthy state. Such professionals also use it to help their clients achieve a Zen state.

The concept of qi isn't exclusive to ancient Chinese culture. In the Yogic or Ayurvedic tradition, this energy or life force is called prana, but people sometimes confuse chi with qi. So, which is which?

While they both refer to the same thing, many use one term over the other depending on the context of the discussion. In terms of restoring a person's balance, qi is the better term to use because it is the physical or nourishing aspect of the food we eat, the water we drink, and the air we breathe. Experts often use qis as their reference when referring to the vital fluids and the energy that circulates inside our bodies. Regardless, both have the same ultimate goal: helping you achieve optimal physical and mental health every day.

What makes qi very important for our health? It's what flows through our bodies via the meridians, and it is responsible for our blood circulation. When our blood and qi move throughout the body properly, we experience optimal health and harmony. In ancient Chinese culture, qi is considered as the energy derived from food and drinks, and a type of gas or pressure that promotes adequate movement inside our bodies.

If optimal health and balance are the byproducts of a balanced qi, the opposite indicates deficiencies in the same. You may develop qi deficiencies through any of the following, individually or in combination:

1. Dirty water

2. Lack of quality sleep

3. Polluted air

4. Poor diet

5. Lack of nutrients or other physical elements for optimal health and performance

Your qi may also become deficient when you don't stimulate your mind sufficiently, if you get insufficient love from others, and if you don't get enough social interactions.

How does qi deficiency manifest itself? Some signs include:

1. Chronic pain

2. Depression

3. Fatigue

4. Feeling chronically stressed

5. Frequent weakness of the muscles

6. Hormonal imbalances

7. Irritability

8. Lethargy

9. Regular cramping

It may be tempting to think the more, the merrier with your qi. Nothing can be further from the truth. For optimal health and wellbeing, balance is key. That is why it is also possible to have excess qi and fall short of optimal physical, mental, and emotional health.

What factors contribute to accumulating excess qi? The most common ones include:

1. Chronic stress

2. Environmental toxins such as air and water pollutants

3. Excess physical activity, i.e., chronic overexertion

4. Overeating

5. Toxic emotions

Balancing Your Qi

Fortunately, achieving the right qi levels isn't rocket science. You can choose from various mind-body practices and techniques, from Qigong and tai chi to reiki and massages. The simplest way to rebalance and keep your qi that way is to avoid over exhausting yourself and getting enough quality sleep regularly. Other practical ways to achieve and maintain your qi balance include acupuncture and movement-based hobbies that promote stretching of the muscles and improved blood flow throughout the body.

If you suffer from imbalanced qi, do your best to identify its reason instead of just trying to alleviate its symptoms. Imbalanced qi is caused by many factors, from dirty air and water to unhealthy food and chronic stress. That's why a healthy, balanced diet and getting adequate rest regularly are key to achieving and maintaining qi balance.

The Five Elements Framework

With Chinese culture, the five elements serve as important foundational pieces for many areas of people's lives. These elements are earth, water, air, fire, and metal. It's no surprise that the five elements framework also plays a crucial role in the Qigong practice, particularly in achieving balance for optimal health and wellbeing.

These five elements provide a comprehensive system of organizing all-natural phenomena in the world into major patterns or groups in nature. Each element falls into specific seasons, directions, climates, stages of life, internal organs, emotions, and many others that are important in our lives. The categories are practically limitless, and these five elements, as taught in Chinese culture, provide a thorough understanding of natural laws and universal order.

When you understand the five elements framework, you'll see the relationship between your body and nature and, more importantly, how the different dimensions of your relating to and affect each other. As you start studying or learning the five elements framework, you must focus on the fact this multi-dimensional perspective of life can provide you with a diagnostic template by which you can learn to spot imbalances in your body, emotions, mind, and spirit. The more you're able to do this, the easier it will be for you to correct any imbalances quickly before they worsen. This framework includes your key internal organs and their relationships with each other pertaining to optimal health and wellbeing.

The five elements of framework or theory can tell you a lot about the environment you're in. For one, it can show you how all things are connected. Let's take water, for example.

According to ancient Chinese culture, water is related to several things, including fear, the kidneys, the color black, winter, cold climates, and the north. During winters, the environmental essence is cold, which impacts and is related to the kidney in several ways. Fear is also linked to cold and the kidneys, albeit in subtle and inconspicuous ways at times.

Air, water, earth, fire, and metal also show you your body's systems and structures and how they relate to each other. These can show you how you are connected to your environment and the natural world at large and how the world is part of the entire universe. While many people these days have severed their connection to nature, the universal idea of interconnection remains valid, nonetheless.

Balance

You may consider the five elements as the basic energies of mother nature in motion. They aren't static, but rather dynamic relationships exist between them all. The two fundamental relationships that govern them our generation and support. Unless these two are balanced, it may be very hard or even impossible to achieve optimal health and wellbeing.

What does generation mean? This refers to a relationship that results in continuous growth. A good picture of the generation is that of a mother and a child. After giving birth, the mother provides her baby with nutrients through her breast milk and other external resources, ensuring her child's survival and growth. This type of relationship can be seen between the liver and kidneys, where the kidney helps generate the liver.

And when we talk about support in the context of the five elements, we talk about a specific type of relationship - one that helps restrict or restrain that energy or force of the others to ensure growth at the right pace. Growing too fast or too slow, too strong or too weak, can lead to major imbalances that can hinder you from achieving optimal health and wellbeing.

Types of Qi

Inside your body, there are two general types or classifications of qi: pre-natal and post-natal.

Pre-Natal Qi

Also called the "source qi," it refers to the vital energy that both parents give to their babies at birth. You may think of it as a person's essence or basic matter, which is the native force supporting the body's tissues and organs. This energy is directly linked to the primary, and most important energy center in the human body called the Ming Men and the body's Eight Extraordinary Vessels.

Post-Natal Qi

On the other hand, this type of energy is a combination of qi you can get from the food and drinks you consume and the air you breathe. It's directly linked to the 12 primary organ systems or meridians of your body. When combined with the pre-natal qi, they create your body's true qi, i.e., the source of energy you use in daily living.

Impact of Qigong

The primary reasons for developing Qigong are balancing, enhancing, and harmonizing the true qi for optimal health, longevity, and spiritual development. Regularly practicing Qigong can lead to direct and positive impacts on the key factors that affect your health and wellbeing: pre-natal qi, post-natal qi, essence, and spirit. These work together and can help oversee your life activities and connect you to the divine.

The Yin and the Yang

One of the most popular concepts in Chinese culture, these two represent the two foundational aspects of all things that exist. Interdependent and complementary, you may think of yin and yang as the foundational relationships the run through everything. When one or both of these are imbalanced, you may suffer from illnesses because you can experience health and well-being when yin and yang are balanced.

The best way to describe the properties of these two is those of fire and water. Yin refers to water, and yang refers to fire. Several qualities that best describe the yin are those that can be said of water:

1. Cold

2. Contracting

3. Dim

4. Fall season

5. Internal

6. Night

7. Thinking

8. Winter season

In relation to your body, it is the bottom, front, right side, and interior parts. The viscera is your inside yin while the earth is your outside one.

But the qualities that can best describe young are those related to fire, such as

1. Bright

2. Daytime

3. Expanding

4. External

5. Hot

6. Rising

7. Spring season

8. Summer season

As it relates to your body, the yang relates to the top, back, left side, and outside. Your bubbles may be considered your inside yang, while heaven is your outside yang.

Being closely connected and interdependent, yin and yang can affect each other when imbalanced. They are deeply involved in all aspects of your life, and to enjoy optimal health and well-being, both must be in a state of balance. Sickness can result from an imbalance in either or both. Once the two have become completely separated, death is the result.

Jing (Body Energy)

Being one of the three treasures of Qigong, jing has no direct translation in the English language. The best English definition often used to describe this treasure is "essence." This is because jing is what really comprises a person, including you, even before your birth.

Many people consider jing as DNA. This is because as DNA's double-strand helix genetic blueprints determine your physiological and energy characteristics before birth, jing does the same as the essence or substance that makes up who you are.

In ancient traditional Chinese medicine philosophy, people believe that all people have a set amount of jing when they're born. Healthy babies have their entire lives to manage the jing they're born with, just like how people budget their inheritance or savings upon retirement. Basically, jing goes inside the body and permanently anchors all the energy people will need throughout their lives.

Now, you may be wondering: why should you bother about caring for your jing when you basically can do nothing about it, given you just inherit it? In other words, why even bother learning about and managing it if you have no say as to the amount you get upon birth?

Now that is a good question! And the answer is simple: doing so can help you "budget" you're jing such that you can live the longest and healthiest life possible. If you spend too much of it as you would with overspending your money, it will quickly run out, and when this happens, your life is over as you know it.

To be able to effectively "budget" or manage your jing supply, you must know the things that can drain it. A few ways that your essence can leak from your body include:

1. A highly stressful lifestyle

2. Being frequently angry

3. Chronic sleep deprivation

4. Substance abuse

5. Too much ejaculation

More than just being aware of what can cause your jinx to leak excessively from your body, you also have to recognize when it is happening. Several of the most common red flags indicative of excessive jing-leaking include:

1. Chronic inability to focus

2. Feeling and looking tired throughout the day

3. Feeling that you're living life without purpose

4. Hair loss

5. You look older than you are or premature aging

In theory, your immune system may be compromised when your jing is wasted or is leaking excessively. This means you can be more vulnerable to sicknesses and diseases. If you're able to care for and manage your jing wisely, you'll be able to boost your immune system, and your body won't easily fall prey to flu, colds, allergies, and the like.

And lastly, you also need to learn how to preserve or even replenish your essence to live the longest and healthiest life possible. One of the best ways you can do these is by eating the right foods, which include:

1. Bee pollen

2. Black rice

3. Bone broth

4. Internal organ meats

5. Kidney beans

6. Poultry and fish eggs

7. Royal jelly

8. See vegetables

9. Seeds

You may also use Chinese herbs that may help replenish your essence. These include mulberry, goji berry, he shou wu, and shan yao. Other ways you can preserve or replenish your jing include:

1. Acupuncture

2. Engaging in regular qi-building exercises like Qigong and tai chi

3. Minimizing sexual intercourse or masturbation

4. Regular meditation

Your Jing, Blood, and Kidneys

One of the worst things you can do for your jing is eating a standard American diet known as SAD. There is a good reason it's called sad!

Today, the average American diet is too high on junk and processed foods, so major illnesses and conditions such as heart problems and cancers are becoming even more prevalent among the population. Coupled with a lack of regular exercise and chronic high-stress levels, these can wreak havoc on any person's jing.

Now, how is jing related to your blood? Excessive jing leaking due to poor diet, sedentary lifestyles, and chronic stress can negatively affect your body's ability to produce blood. Based on ancient traditional Chinese medicine theories, the jing is stored in a person's kidneys, from which it travels to the bone and ultimately becoming bone marrows. As we all know, blood is produced in the bone marrow.

And speaking of chronic stress as one of the critical jing-leaking factors, how does it contribute to the leaking? For this, it's important to understand a theory called the adrenal fatigue theory.

In western functional medicine, it is believed that adrenal fatigue is caused by chronic excess cortisol levels, which is a stress hormone. In turn, cortisol tends to flood the body when under chronically high levels of stress. When this happens, a person's hormonal, metabolic pathways are both diverted and disrupted in response to the need to produce more cortisol.

Now here's the interesting part: cortisol is produced by the adrenal glands, which coincidentally rests on top of the kidneys. If the adrenal glands are overworked, it also negatively affects the kidneys, in which jing is stored. This is why chronically excessive stress levels can lead to excessive leaking of the jing via wreaking havoc on the kidneys.

Your Essence and Your Brain

Excessively leaking jing isn't just bad for your kidneys and blood. It can also negatively affect your brain.

Based on traditional Chinese medicine, your brain contains a sea of marrow, and if too much essence is leaking from you, your kidneys become weak and eventually lead to malnourishment of your brain. When this happens, telltale signs include the inability to concentrate, poor memory, brain fog, and confusion.

Working Together With Your Qi and Shen

Inside your body, jing is the densest physical matter, and it determines who and what you are, just like DNA. Based on traditional Chinese medicine, your essence nourishes, cools, and fuels your body. When you live a moderate or healthy lifestyle, which includes getting enough rest, a healthy diet, and adequate stress management, you don't just help preserve or replenish your jing but also support your qi.

And when you're able to manage and contain your essence without excessive leaks properly, you enjoy abundant levels of qi. When both of these are optimal, you may expect your spirit or your shen to be optimal.

And speaking of which...

Shen (Spiritual Energy)

The last of the three treasures of Qigong refers to the energy of your heart. In traditional Chinese medicine, this is represented by the fire element. As a form of energy, your shen directly connects with those of your spleen and livers.

Your qi relates to your vital energy and breath, both of which animate you as a person. But your jing is the energy you get from the foods and drinks you consume and the air you breathe, both of which constitute your physical essence. How is your shen related to your qi and jing? Your shen comes from the latter two, and in turn, it gives energy to your qi.

Sources of Shen

Your shen energy has two sources: pre-natal and post-natal. Your pre-natal shen, as the term implies, is that which you were born with. Your energy connects with the internal aspect of the universe, also called the Tao. When you're familiar with or know the concept of shen, you'll be able to connect with what it's called in TCM as the mind of the Tao or of the universe. This is permanent and may be considered as your eternal soul, but you may find it difficult to recognize because of how your mind has been conditioned from childhood.

As the name implies, too, post-natal shen is that which you're able to derive or acquire after being born. Where do you get this? Your jing and qi.

Your post-natal shen can be directly shaped or influenced by the environment in which you live, the habits you develop, and mental conditioning. Basically, it's directly formed by your external environment and your own thoughts and behaviors. Speaking of thoughts, chronic overthinking, as with any excessive behavior, may prematurely exhaust your shen or even lead to disconnection from your pre-natal one.

The Five Elements and Your Shen

All five organs are responsible for containing (or *housing*) your shen. Your heart is the primary container; all of your other internal organs, including their related energies, can affect your shen. It's because every organ in your body contains a part or area of your being, which in turn can impact your physical, mental, and spiritual wellbeing. This is why in traditional Chinese medicine, balancing the body's energies is crucial, non-negotiable even, for optimal health and wellbeing, both physical and spiritual.

Because your shen is the energy of your heart, it helps you achieve a healthy balance between your mind and your emotions. Your emotions can help regulate your reasoning and vice versa. To a great extent, you'd be right to assume that it helps you manage your consciousness.

Your shen may also be the path to your spirit, which sets you apart from animals. When you're able to balance your shen regularly, it'll be natural for you to follow the rhythms of the universe and the laws of nature. A healthy and balanced shen means a joy-filled life.

On the other hand, excessive and uncontrollable emotions may lead to an unbalanced shen. If you cannot handle them, the challenges in your life may lead to nervous tension, sleeplessness, and anxiety. Some ways you can tell if this is already happening is a profound and chronic sense of sadness, restlessness, and chronic fatigue.

Balancing Your Shen

If you find yourself disconnected from your post-natal shen or the mind of the Tao, one way you can reconnect with it is through regular meditation. You can also reconnect with your tranquil and empowering inner space by getting regular sleep and through centered prayers.

Externally, you may utilize specific herbs to balance your shen. These include reishi mushrooms and gotu kola, but before supplementing your daily regimen with such herbs, first consult with a professional herbalist or a medical professional. This is especially important if preexisting medical conditions require maintenance medications or if you're pregnant or nursing.

Chapter 3: The Three Intentful Corrections: Body, Breath, and Mind

One of the most important things you must know about the practice of Qigong is the foundational concept of the three *intentful* corrections. In particular, these refer to important corrections that need to be made about your body, the way you breathe, and mental focus or mind. These corrections need to be made because any imbalances in these key areas can keep you from optimizing the benefits of the practice.

Fortunately, these three intentful corrections aren't difficult. You need not be very strict about following them because they are more focused on paying close attention to your body and doing your best to live as healthy as possible.

Your Body

When it comes to your body, the corrections pertain to your posture. This, together with routing and stances, are crucial for ensuring the balanced circulation of your qi. When your posture isn't correct, the flow of your qi can be disrupted.

When you start practicing Qigong, you will assume stationary and moving postures. Regardless of if you are standing up or sitting down, you'd want to be as tall and straight as possible. Doing this helps give your organs more working room and enable your bones to hold you up more easily. When you stand up or sit down straight, your spine's bones can stack perfectly on top of each other to provide maximum support for your body. Whenever you slouch, most of the work to keep you from tipping over goes to your muscles. This can either fatigue you more quickly, lead to muscle strain and tightness, or both.

One thing to consider so you always be conscious of assuming a straight and upward position, whether sitting down or standing up, is that the head is heavy. The inability to maintain a straight and upward posture can cause a forward-positioned head, which is common among senior citizens. When you bring your head up and slightly back, you may relieve your neck and shoulders of the strain of having to hold it up.

Sitting in a slouched position has other disadvantages, too. In such a position, you tend to pack or compress your organs together. When this happens, you may impede their optimal function. Blood and other body fluid circulation may also be limited when your organs are compressed together. When you sit with good posture, you're not just able to optimize organ functions and bodily fluid circulation; you may strengthen your weak core muscles, too. So, sitting up properly, i.e., in a straight and upright posture, can help make your body stronger too. This is even more important because most of the time, you're just sitting down.

Now, let's talk about standing up. Most people tend to stand with their pelvises tilted too far forward. Especially in senior citizens, this creates a "swayback," which isn't healthy for the lower back. An easy way to restore the pelvis back into a neutral position is by imagining your tailbone being pulled down by a weight. This helps you create a pelvic ball that can properly hold your digestive organs, help you become more stable and grounded, and even look thinner.

Another important posture you must learn when exercising Qigong is to avoid pulling yourself up using your shoulders or chest. The proper posture should be having the shoulders always relaxed, hanging down, and slightly drawn back. An easy way to do this is to imagine a string tied to the top of your head and being pulled upward. This helps you stretch and lengthen your spine, which can help you look thinner, even taller. More importantly, it decompresses your internal organs and gives them more room to work optimally.

Your joints also play an important role in assuming proper posture in Qigong. In particular, you must keep your joints soft and bent slightly when performing the exercise. They should neither be tight nor locked.

With your arms, they should be shaped like a bow. As far as your legs go, they should be slightly bent at the knees. If your leg and core muscles aren't strong enough yet, you may need more time to practice these and strengthen them. The best way to strengthen these muscles is to simply use them the way nature designed them to be used: with good posture and gentle movements.

Speaking of movements, they're slow and flowing when doing Qigong. More than just being easy on your joints, slow movements also help strengthen your muscles. In particular, your arm and leg muscles need to work against gravity when slowly lifting and bringing down the arm and upper body, respectively. Because of the slow movements, it's like you're performing resistance or lifting exercises using your body weight. Hence, performing Qigong correctly may help strengthen your upper and lower bodies, as well as your core muscles, without straining your joints.

But the flowing, repetitive nature of the movements can help you learn to relax better by activating your parasympathetic nervous system. This is because a few of the movements involved are like rocking ourselves to sleep. So more than just strength and flexibility benefits, Qigong can help you lower your stress and even facilitate healing in several areas of your health. To that extent, the overall impact of exercise on your health and wellbeing is more important than the practice itself.

When performing Qigong movements, consider these basic guidelines:

1. Each exercise provides numerous options, from sitting down to walking, which helps you do Qigong in ways that are most appropriate for your current physical fitness level.

2. If you are assisting others, don't grab them by their wrist but instead offer your hands.

3. Keep your range of movements within your comfort zone and avoid overstretching because pain isn't necessary to enjoy the practice's benefits.

4. The practice's primary goal is relaxation, so always try to have fun and relax instead of stressing over the movements.

5. You don't have to be rigid or strict about the exercises, and you can modify them according to your specific needs or conditions.

6. You don't have to perform exercises perfectly to enjoy their benefits because the important thing is to continue doing something rather than nothing.

Your Breathing

You may be wondering, is there actually a right way of breathing and, by extension, a wrong way of doing it? If you're alive, doesn't that mean you're breathing the right way already?

To clarify, the second intentful correction, your breathing, doesn't mean the way you're breathing is wrong. Otherwise, you wouldn't get enough oxygen and die of asphyxiation eventually.

What is meant by correcting your breathing is working on how you breathe to maximize both the quantity and quality of air that goes into your body. In short, it's a transition from sub-optimal breathing to an optimal one.

So, what does sub-optimal breathing look like? The simplest way to describe it is chest breathing, where a person uses muscles between the ribs to suck air into the lungs' upper regions. This breathing type may be considered relatively shallow because it only fills the upper part of the lungs with air, failing to maximize their full capacities.

In Qigong, you'll learn to transition from chest breathing to belly breathing. This type of breathing involves slow and deep breaths that fill your entire lungs from the bottom up. This is the optimal form and intentful correction of the breath.

If you are used to just breathing, you'll immediately feel the difference when you start to take deep and slow belly breaths. Researchers have noted that as few as ten deep and slow belly breaths a day can help you achieve a 10 to 30% improvement in vitality and physical endurance. If as simple as ten of these can help you significantly change how you feel and, in your energy, can you imagine if you make this your normal breathing habit?

Deep belly breaths can help you relax so much better and much faster. Scientifically speaking, breathing this way helps slow down the heart rate. This is why people are often instructed to take slow and deep breaths whenever they feel anxious or nervous. It isn't a coincidence that one of the physical symptoms of anxiety, stress, and nervousness is shallow and rapid breaths, usually via the chest.

Ideally, you should use your diaphragm muscles to generate the necessary pressure for drawing oxygen into your lungs. When you take a deep breath, your torso expands in six different directions simultaneously. As you do this, your body's pressure change helps move the lymph and other bodily fluids through your tissues. Your internal organs experience a delicate rolling motion massage every time you breathe deeply through your belly. These are some of their reasons deep belly breaths are very helpful to heal the body on many levels.

And another way of breathing that can help you release emotional tension is moans and sighs. The Qigong exercise call "lazy monkey wakes up" uses moaning or sighing to release tension from the body. This exercise also uses the sound "ha" as a toning form for breaking up stagnation and congestion in the chest area. Another popular way of breathing that helps release tension, specifically from the shoulders, is laughing.

Another way that slow and deep belly breaths help you relax is by calming your mind. Remember how people tend to breathe fast and shallowly when very stressed and nervous? By slowing down and deepening your breaths, you'll be able to hit two birds with one stone: deeper breaths and slower heart rate. Together, these can help you alleviate stress and anxiety symptoms and, ultimately, calm your mind. As an ancient eastern saying goes, "the mind rides on the breath as a rider does on a horse." This is why you need to learn to control your breathing. Doing so also helps you control your mind.

Your Mind

Your mind, specifically mental focus, is the final intentful correction that needs to be addressed for optimal Qigong practice. The best mindset you can have to get the most out of the exercise is to be present, centered, and always aware of when your mind strays away from the moment.

Let's face it, most of us tend to spend much of our days either thinking about the past or worrying about the future. Not that these are bad but overdoing them can prevent optimal health and wellbeing. It's all right to think of these things now and then, but if they occupy our mind most of the time, it's neither healthy nor productive. That is why in Qigong, it is important to be continuously aware of focusing on the present moment.

When you shift your focus to the present moment during Qigong, you can let old grudges go and set aside anxieties and fears, even if only for the moment. Because you need to focus on gentle movements and proper breathing while performing Qigong, you'll be able to train your mind to focus on the present moment and let go of past and future concerns. More importantly, your ability to do so can help you experience the joys and peace of the moment.

For most people, their attention is fixed on what's happening in their external environment. Chances are, they're always on the lookout for incoming "attacks" on them, such as criticisms, mistakes, unhappiness, blame, and even finding that one person who will complete them. If this is you, you can find solace in the fact that Qigong can help you regain your inner balance by shifting your focus inside you instead of outside. By focusing your attention on your breaths and movements, you can train your mind to focus on the present much better and ultimately achieve balance.

Especially for people living in the United States or other western countries, over-analysis seems to be a common habit. Many troublesome thoughts run through their heads and rob them of their joy, such as

1. Am I ever going to find the one true love that will make me complete?

2. Do I look fat in this shirt?

3. What are the chances I'll fail in this endeavor?

4. When will I ever achieve financial abundance?

5. Why the hell did I even think about doing that?

In Qigong, you'll be encouraged to bring your mental awareness or focus back to your chest area, where the heart center or the heart-mind resides. When you're able to do this regularly, you'll be able to harness fresh mental resources for solving problems as they arise. This is only possible when you're able to slow down the needless mental chatter in your mind. Regularly practicing Qigong is an excellent way of achieving this.

When it comes to intently correcting your mind or focus, grounding is very important. This refers to being connected to the earth. Learning to focus on the moment can help you go outside of your head and become increasingly aware not just of your body and its movements but also of its connection to the planet.

Think about it: why does walking in nature trails or hiking in the mountains feel so relaxing and invigorating? It's because these are a few of the most effective ways of connecting with the earth, a.k.a., grounding. Through regular Qigong practice, you'll be able to achieve the same connection to the earth. How?

According to traditional Chinese medicine, you can do this by focusing on how your pelvis is currently tilted. When you're able to achieve the right pelvic tilt, you'll also be able to open up your groin area. When these happen, your legs start to feel more connected to the flow of your body and its movements and, eventually, establish a genuine connection with nature.

When you're able to focus your mind on the present moment, you'll be able to notice everything within and around you. Then, you'll be able to enjoy the now and feel one with the earth.

Movement Principles

As mentioned earlier, the movements involved in Qigong are easy, smooth, flowing, very deliberate, and slow. You must always remember not the overdo the movements to avoid straining or injuring muscles or joints. Again, the emphasis is on movement within your physical comfort zone with just enough stretch, which should never feel painful.

As with the movements, breathe deeply, smoothly, and deeply. Your breathing must also be coordinated with your movements. With movement and breathing coordination, the general principle is to breathe in as you relax your muscles and breathe out as you contract them or as you lower your body.

Mentally speaking, you must focus on the moment by paying close attention to how you execute your movements and coordinating it with your breathing. This is one crucial aspect that differentiates Qigong from other forms of exercise. As long as you do this, you'll be able to keep your mind centered on the moment. Eventually, your focus will be directed inwardly so you can be keenly aware of what's going on in your body.

Deep and slow breathing. Repeatedly performing slow and flowing movements. Meditative focus. Together, these three elements synergistically stimulate your body's relaxation response as a means of reversing the negative effects of aging, stress, and promoting healing.

Chapter 4: Standing Qigong: Stances, Posture, and Balance

Now, we are ready to talk about how to practice Qigong. In this chapter, you will learn the basics of performing standing Qigong, specifically stances, posture, and balance.

Warming Up

As with any type of physical exercise, warming up is highly recommended. While Qigong isn't as strenuous or impactful as most other types of exercises, it still involves movements that stretch your muscles and joints. Without proper warmup, you increase your risks for overstretching or straining. Here's how you can start warming up for every session:

1. Warm up by performing ankle circles. Follow them up with nice circles and, finally, hip circles. Do at least nine circles each to warm up properly.

2. Next, warm and loosen up your shoulders. Do this by rolling your shoulders up, back, and down for at least eight repetitions. Follow it up with rolling the same up, forward, and down for at least eight reps, too.

3. Then, move on to your neck. Gently roll it clockwise and reverse the movement by rolling it counterclockwise after one repetition or one full round. To roll it, start by dropping your head forward, then rolling it gently to your right, to the back (your face should be facing upward at this point), to the left, and stopping when it returns to your starting point. Reverse the movement to perform a counterclockwise roll.

4. Finally, warm up your arms. Begin by putting your right hand behind your right shoulder as you breathe in. Your right elbow should be pointing upward and forming a peak at this point.

5. While holding your breath, put your left hand on the right elbow.

6. As you breathe out, gently push down your right elbow to slide your right hand as far down your back as comfortably possible for a light stretch. As you release the push, breathe in again. Do this at least two more times before switching to the other arm for at least three repetitions.

When you're done with the warmup, you may now perform the exercise.

Postures

One of the most enduring forms of Qigong, one that has withstood the test of time, involves standing in a wide variety of postures. Most Qigong practitioners continue doing these because it's believed to be a very effective way to improve one's energy and health. It's not just limited to those. Some traditional forms of Chinese martial arts also incorporate specific standing Qigong postures for developing strength and power.

In Qigong, the standing postures used aren't just based on a thorough understanding of the physical body but also of the life force energy that animates every living thing on earth, i.e., the qi. With good standing postures, relaxation is important because when both mind and body are relaxed, qi can flow optimally throughout the body.

Standing Qigong postures are often thought of as the naturally fluid model of the human body because of their natural focus on fluidity or flow of movements and relaxation. Once you start assuming these standing postures, you'll be able to tell how different they are from what we know to be as "good posture" today - shoulders pulled back, just lifted up, legs straight, and the chin raised.

Two important principles involved in Qigong are balance and relaxation. When you're able to balance your body through natural alignment, you need minimum muscular tension just to be able to maintain an upright standing position. This helps minimize or greatly reduce muscular fatigue and strain, allowing you to perform Qigong more efficiently.

For learning proper Qigong posture, you must understand that it's not something you'll be able to do instantly. It's because you probably developed sub-optimal postural habits from the time you were a child until adulthood. Given these habits took time to develop, you may also take time to relearn a natural and optimal posture. So, you shouldn't be rushing it, but instead, understand and accept that the Qigong way of doing this is to peel away accumulated postural habits one at a time, layer by layer.

Another important thing you must learn about proper Qigong posture is the 70% principle. This means you shouldn't force your body to do something beyond its current capacity, but instead, use no more than up to 70% of its capacity.

Remember that just as with anything worth doing or achieving, learning how to strike the proper standing postures in Qigong will require time and practice. If you go beyond your body's 70% capacity or worse, go beyond 100%, you won't achieve relaxation during the practice, and worse, you may injure yourself through things like overstretching.

Remember, take your time and always be cognizant that relaxation is a key factor or component of the practice.

Basic Standing Posture Alignments

These alignments start with your feet, as they are the foundation for any standing postures. Also, you may use them every day if you think they can be beneficial for you.

Feet Apart

Begin by standing with both feet about hip or shoulder-width apart. This means your feet must be beneath either your shoulders or your hips in this position.

The primary reason for this posture or alignment is to let your leg bones line up so that your muscles can be as relaxed as possible when you lower your body to the ground. If you try a much wider stance, you risk putting more work or tension on your muscles as you lower your body closer to the ground.

Parallel Feet

Bring your feet as close auras parallel to each other as comfortably possible. If your usual standing position has your feet turned in or out, it may take you a while to learn and adjust to this new stance. The important thing here is not to force and rush your feet in positions either strenuous or painful. Doing so only puts you at risk for injuries to your feet, hips, knees, or other body parts. So, always remember the 70% rule and proceed gradually.

Knees Slightly Bent

Instead of keeping your knees locked while standing, keep them slightly bent such that you can bounce your body up and down gently, such that your knee joints feel springy instead of rigid. Be careful not to bend the knees too much because doing so run you the risk of pushing your knees forward, which may transfer a lot of your body weight to your leg muscles. But locking your knee joints deprives them of "springiness," which is important for reducing or eliminating much of the impact or strain from them.

Lengthened Spine

Gently elevate the top of your head to "stretch" both your neck and your spine. If you are unfamiliar with how this is done, just imagine somebody gently lifting your head up by pulling on both your ears. Another way you can do this is by putting your thumbs beneath your skull, just under your ears, and lightly push your head up to elongate your spine.

Remember, the operative word here is "gently." If you push or pull too hard, you may tense your muscles such that relaxation, which is one of the important guiding principles of Qigong, becomes impossible.

Chin Slightly Sunk

Contrary to the modern perception of excellent posture, you must be cognizant not to lift your chin to appear taller. It's because doing so reduces the length of your nape, which may excessively curve your cervical spine. Remember that while lengthening the back of the neck is important, it shouldn't be at the expense of a curved spine.

Broad and Relaxed Shoulders

Instead of pulling your shoulders all the way back, allow them to naturally broaden sideward or outward. To do this, let them relax as much as possible and let gravity pull them down naturally. Next, gently broaden them from your sternum and spine to the tips of your shoulders.

If you follow your shoulder girdle's natural shape, your shoulders will broaden in a slightly concave manner instead of a straight line. To achieve the length you're after, follow your body's natural curves. Take note: this isn't the same as rounding your shoulders by collapsing it forward, like what you see with most people we have been working in front of their computers all day.

Empty Chest

In ancient tai chi tradition, there's a saying that goes like this: the spine lifts, and the chest empties into the belly. So, allow your chest to sink a little and stay soft instead of lifting it and letting it stick out. Just remember that the keyword phrase here is "sink a little" and not "collapse." You'll know if you're doing it right if this feels light.

This is encouraged for several good reasons, but the most important one is to relax your chest enough such that your qi can circulate efficiently down to the front of your body. This is because, based on ancient traditional Chinese medicine, stress and anxiety result from energy rising up to the front of a person's body and, in the process, getting stuck inside the chest and the head. Together with broadening your shoulders, thinking your chest slightly allows the back of your lungs to have more space to move when you breathe and facilitate efficient circulation of your energy down to the front of your body.

Let Go of the Pelvis

Last, let gravity sink your pelvis' big and heavy bones. When we talk about letting go of the pelvis, we're not talking about positioning your pelvis in a certain way. It's more about relaxing or releasing the muscles that hold it in position. Instead of tilting or tucking your pelvis, you'll be able to find its natural or neutral position by letting go of the muscles.

Be Patient

Always remember that as an adult, you have a lot of set ways of doing things. This includes your posture. You will need enough time and consistent effort to learn and be able to maintain these important alignments at the same time. More so while feeling relaxed. Because it'll take your mind and body enough time to adjust, you must be patient with yourself. One of the worst things you can do is rush yourself into mastering these alignments simultaneously. Remember, Rome wasn't built in a day, but they were busy laying bricks by the hour. So, be patient.

Qigong Stances

With Qigong, the five basic stances you need to learn include:

1. The Ma Bu, better known as the horse stance

2. The Gong Bu or the bow and arrow stance

3. The Xie Bu or the twisted stance

4. The Pu Bu or the sliding stance

5. The Xu Bu, better known as the empty stance

The Horse Stance

This is also called the *horse-riding stance*, and is one of the most popular basic stances in Qigong and Chinese martial arts in general. As you may glean from the name itself, this posture is akin to the one riding the back of a horse.

The more you research about this specific Qigong stance, you'll discover that they are a myriad number of variations of this. As such, I discourage obsessing about finding the one true or legitimate way of doing the horse stance. It's because certain variations are more appropriate than the others depending on the specific type of Qigong or Chinese martial arts you're performing. Still, all variations adhere to certain basic rules, and you must know why you're practicing Qigong, how you're doing it, and its basic theoretical foundations. The deeper your understanding of the horse stance, the better you'll be able to tweak it according to your goals, preferences, and needs.

What is the importance of the horse stance in Qigong? Normally, this is used in martial arts as an effective and efficient way of shifting from one technique or form to another. Practitioners use it specifically for developing stability, centering, and rooting or grounding. When it comes to Qigong, three of the most important foundations are stability, center, and roots. It can also be used for developing strength in the back, waist, and leg muscles.

Another important reason for using the horse stance when practicing Qigong is that it is a relaxed and comfortable posture that helps achieve a smooth flow of qi. As such, you'll need to learn how to assume this stance with minimal muscle support and using mostly your body's structure.

Later on, you will also use the three foundations of stability, center, and roots when assuming other narrower postures or stances. This will allow you to stand in a relaxed and strain-free manner for long periods, especially when doing stationary Qigong or standing meditations. In turn, you'll be able to feel comfortable and enable your qi to circulate freely.

When you learn to master the horse stance and practice regularly, you can also align your lower body much better. It's because the ma bu stance is the perfect stance for relaxing and aligning both your pelvis and legs. This realignment process needs time to complete, and initially, you will learn to relax your body from the outside in. As you do this, you'll first be able to release superficial tensions normally associated with larger muscle groups like the legs. Eventually, you learn to achieve relaxation in your deeper muscles and for the tendons, ligaments, fascia, etc.

If you look at this alignment process, it involves many baby steps or smaller alignments inside your body. When your body is relaxed, the many small corrections can appear to happen spontaneously because these small alignment processes naturally occur in your body when it's not strained or under tension. In this stance, you'll be able to slowly learn how to get in touch with your body tissues and structures. More importantly, you'll develop the ability to sense how interconnected they all are.

The ma bu or horse stance has its own set of characteristics, but many of these are not as obvious as they seem. That is why, as a beginner, I highly recommend applying them one at a time instead of all at once. Learning the horse stance requires patient practice and the gradual deepening of knowledge.

Let's talk about your feet first. Begin by standing with both feet at approximately twice the shoulder-width apart. Also, they should be parallel to each other, with the second toe pointing forward. Always be mindful about your feet staying flat on the ground while practicing the stance.

While you're in a horse stance, your body weight must be evenly distributed on both feet. You must use your center of gravity (the area of your lower Dantian) as the transmission point for your weight, from which it will move down to your legs. The end destination is the yong quan points of your feet. This is crucial because by doing it this way, your lower back is relaxed. Assuming this stance with a tight or tense lower back area may cause tension in the said area.

Initially, it'll feel like you're leaning a bit forward. As you practice this, you'll be able to develop the appropriate feeling.

Now, let's turn to your knees. They must be bent up an angle such that they line up vertically with your toes. To do this, gently push your knees outward in a sideways direction to align them as much as possible with your feet. Remember that discomfort, strain, or pain indicate that you are not doing it properly.

When you try to transition to a much wider stance, achieving the same level of alignment can be a bit more challenging and may take a bit more time in practice. The important thing is you're able to do it properly, so take your time mastering the position. If you insist on adopting a lower or wider stance without mastering knee alignment, you increase your risk for any injuries over time.

Speaking of a wider stance, double shoulder width is common in most martial arts and even in martial Qigong, but popular doesn't necessarily mean you should do it. How do you know how wide your stance should be? By how you feel.

As soon as you feel discomfort, strain, or pain, regardless of how narrow or wide your stance is, that is your red flag that you should make the necessary adjustments to your stance's width. To determine the appropriate or best one for you, you'll need to try various widths. The one in which you feel most comfortable and relaxed and lets you clearly find your center of gravity is the appropriate choice.

More than just the width of your stance in the ma bu posture, you must also pay attention to its height. This should be based on the kind and style of martial arts you are doing. In general, the deeper the stance is, the stronger your legs can become. That is why very deep ones are often used to develop excellent leg strength.

Going very deep often compromises proper posture or form because of its difficulty level. That is why you must gradually work on deepening your stance rather than going for a very deep one right off the bat. As a beginner, the higher stance versions of the ma bu should be your starting point.

Particularly in the Qigong practice, the height of your stance depends primarily on how you feel. If it is too low or deep, you will cause your leg muscles to tighten up and hinder the flow of your qi to your feet. If you're standing too high as a beginner, you won't be as stable as you haven't developed the necessary roots just yet.

While a higher stance is appropriate for beginners, you shouldn't assume a very high one either. Just high enough to make you feel comfortable without compromising your stability too much. To determine the idea stands hype, you can go lower, but only until the point, you are still comfortable in the legs. By doing this, you'll enjoy optimal stability, and by gradually deepening your stance over time, you can develop stronger leg muscles.

If you eventually want to achieve maximum qi flow through the legs, you must learn higher stances so your leg muscles are as relaxed as possible. As with deep stances, you can achieve stability even at very high stances by developing your roots over time. This is what many of the most experienced practitioners do.

Horse Stance Leg & Pelvic Arch

You can compare your pelvis and legs' structural connections to each other to the arch of stone bridges. If you are not familiar with how they look like, google them now for reference.

Stone bridges are made with such arches to ensure their ability to bear under huge weights that cross it regularly. The prominent stone in the middle of the bridge is called the keystone, and with your lower body, it's the pelvis. Just as stone bridges would collapse without a keystone, your body's structural integrity would be compromised without a healthy functioning pelvis. It bears the weight of the body and your head.

To transfer your upper body's weight down to your legs, you must learn to release the weight from your pelvis. When you're able to do this, you can successfully transition your upper body weight all the way to the ground.

It's easy to know when your lower body isn't aligned properly. You'll feel most of your torso's weight in your lower body, such as your calves, thighs, knees, and hips. You will also notice that your leg and hip muscles are tight because they're trying to maintain the balance of your weight. As mentioned earlier, if your leg muscles are tense, this will also constrict your qi's downward flow to your feet. Aside from that, it can also disrupt the flow of chief from the earth towards her upper body. In short, tense hip and leg muscles can constrict the efficient flow of qi in your body. That is why in Qigong, the emphasis is on keeping your body relaxed during the practice.

You also have to be mindful of going too deep or too low, as with the Shaolin's Horse stance. Why? You risk structural misalignment as your upper body weight tends to push down between your legs. While you may strengthen your legs using very deep stances, the potential tradeoff is the inability to achieve optimal relaxation and, consequently, disrupted qi flow.

All this being said, you'll have an easier time learning how to assume the right pelvic posture by assuming a stance slightly wider than shoulder-width. As you progress in your Qigong beginners' journey, you can adopt a narrower stance, e.g., shoulder width, while still applying the same "arch" rule for the pelvis and the legs.

Your Head, Torso, and Spine

Ideally, your torso must be relaxed, centered, and upright. It's best to have your pelvis relaxed and hanging from your spine's base downwards when assuming the ma bu or horse stance. Your sacrum must neither be tilted forward nor backward, and you can achieve the ideal position by bending your knees and sinking from your kua (your body's energy gates). If you do this, you can achieve a relaxed lower back essential for optimal flowing qi.

The easiest way to achieve torso uprightness, centeredness, and relaxation is by imagining a piece of rope tied to the top of your head, and the other end is being pulled gently upward. This has the effect of gently pulling up your spine to lengthen and open it softly. Always be cognizant that your head must be vertically aligned to the center of your pelvis.

Also, slightly move your chin backward so you can straighten your neck. To do this, imagine pushing the area above your lips backward and, in the process, straightening your neck.

You need to keep your shoulder joints and chest open and relaxed. You may also rest the palms of your hands on your lower Dantian area. Finally, keep the tip of your tongue in contact with the roof of your mouth.

Getting Into the Horse Stance

To learn how to use your mind to lead the flow of your qi down into the earth and build strong energy routes to achieve stability, the ma bu or horse stance is your best bet. Here's how to do it:

1. Stand up with your feet double shoulder with apart. If it makes you feel uncomfortable or strained, you may use a narrower one instead.

2. Ensure both feet are parallel to each other, with the second toe pointing straight ahead.

3. Allow your body weight to descend from your center of gravity through your legs and, ultimately, to the yong quan points of your feet.

4. Keep your knees slightly bent up to where it is vertically aligned with your toes. Do not allow them to go forward beyond the toes.

5. Let your legs and pelvis form an arch as if you are riding on the back of a horse.

6. Relax your lower back and pelvis, with the latter hanging down from the bottom of your spine. Make sure your sacrum is centered, neither tilted forward nor pushed backward.

7. Then imagine somebody pulling a rope upward with the other end tide to the top of your head to gently pull up, lengthen, and open up your spine.

8. Straighten your neck by pushing your chin backward.

9. Relax and open your shoulder joints and chest. Put the palm of your hands on your lower dan tian.

10. Touch the roof of your mouth with the tip of your tongue.

11. Take slow, deep belly breaths and calm your mind.

At first, practice this stands for just a few minutes. You don't want to overwhelm yourself to where you could either get injured, burn out, or both. Just remember that the goal is to stand in a relaxed manner using this stance for at least 20 minutes, and you can accomplish this over time by gradually building up the skill and stamina. The proper form must always take precedence over the duration. Let your feeling of being comfortable and relaxed be your barometer. Just practice consistently every day, even for short periods.

The Bow Stance

After the horse stance, the next one you must learn is the bow stance. This is often used when shifting body weight from one leg to another and when changing our body's direction. As with the horse stance, you can perform this high or low according to how comfortable you feel.

Here are the steps on how to take this stance:

1. One foot is in front of the other

2. The foot in front should face directly forward

3. The front foot's knee must be on top of the foot and should not go beyond the vertical line extending from the toes. This ensures no excess strain is placed on the knee

4. Your hindfoot should face outward to the side at a 45-degree angle

5. Your pelvis must be facing forward

6. Drawback your fists so they'll be in line with your body

The Iron Cross Stance

If your shoulders are tight and if you tend to either slouch or hunch, this is the ideal stance to help you address or correct this posture. Here's how to get into the stance:

> 1. Stand with your feet parallel to each other and up to shoulder width

> 2. Relax your legs

> 3. Tuck your pelvis in as if you are seated on a stool. Doing this helps you to move your body from the waist freely and depressurizes your lower back nerves

> 4. Hold your head high and tuck your chin slightly in. Just imagine it being suspended from the center of the head by a string

> 5. Extend your arms to the side of your body at approximately shoulder height and reach outward. You should resemble a big cross with this stance

Consistency is Key

Fortunately, you need not spend months just to learn how to get into these stances properly. Just need to put in consistent time, attention, and effort in two learning how to perform them comfortably. Even as few as five minutes weekly in each stance can help you develop an awareness of which parts of your body are tense faster than you can imagine. Every breath you take suddenly expands and stretches your body, and with every exhale, you help it relax.

Consistently practicing these will allow you to significantly improve your posture over time and make it more comfortable and easier to hold these stances for longer periods. Eventually, you'll be able to open up your joints and feel more energy flowing in your body as you learn how to relax more and more while in these stances. You can develop the best energy flow through structurally sound and balanced postures by regularly practicing these static exercises.

Chapter 5: Qigong Breathing and Meditation

Two of the most important components of Qigong are the breath and the practice of meditation. In this chapter, we will talk about these two in detail.

Qigong Breathing Exercise Benefits

Qigong philosophy believes that a light heart and a healthy body can be achieved by going back or reclaiming our child-like nature. Instead of becoming more rigid, set in our ways, and stubborn as we grow old, Qigong allows us to achieve greater spontaneity, suppleness, and ability to be receptive as we age. You may picture each child's mind as a clear lake that reflects the sky above. You may achieve the same mental clarity by admitting or accepting that you don't know everything. What you do know may not always be right. Hence the saying "an intelligent person learns something new every day, and a wise person forgets something daily."

Young people live life as if they have limitless energy, but those reserves tend to decrease significantly as they age. The same happens to you, too. To replenish your personal batteries with vitality and regain a clear and open mind, you must practice what is called in Qigong as *the original breath.*

This kind of breathing is performed by breathing deeply like an infant using the lower abdomen. By doing this, you'll be able to redirect your focus away from your head down to your body. As you do this, you'll also be able to pull essential energy from out of the air surrounding you, which can help sustain and nourish your organs.

Qigong, particularly through breathing exercises, can help you focus on specific parts of your body, helping you restore its balance. By doing this, you'll be able to experience significant benefits, both physically and mentally.

One benefit is clearing your bladder meridian. Together with your kidneys, it helps flush out toxins from your body. This alone can be considered a very crucial process for your health and wellbeing.

But not only that, but your bladder's meridian also contributes greatly to your emotional balance. In particular, your bladder meridian emotions can help significantly improve your enthusiasm, self-confidence, and self-expression. It also helps foster intimacy, sexuality, control, and courage.

Considering how important these emotions are, can you imagine the serious emotional repercussions of an imbalanced bladder meridian? Some of these include the inability to make important decisions, jealousy, or anxiety.

This is just one example of an area that Qigong breathing can be most beneficial. It can also help you optimize other internal organs' function, including your spleen meridian and other qi points of your body.

Qigong breathing can help you harmonize your entire body by promoting qi's best flow throughout your body. It can also help you enjoy regular personal quiet time, fostering greater mindfulness and a clear mind. That is why when it comes to Qigong breathing, there's practically no downside.

Qigong Breathing Techniques

The Original Breath

As the name implies, this is the most basic breathing technique you can practice in Qigong. Here's how to do it properly:

1. You can do this by sitting down on a chair or cushion or by standing up. The key is to find the right balance for your spine, i.e., long and stretched yet relaxed. This is important because the flow of your qi is maximized with good posture alignment. On the other hand, access muscular tension associated with perfectionism can significantly constrict your qi's flow.

2. If you choose to perform this while standing up, make sure both your feet are parallel, about shoulder-width apart, and your knees are soft and slightly bent.

3. Next, fold your hands on top of your navel and observe your breathing.

4. Gradually, take longer, deeper, and smoother breaths.

5. Breathe using your lower abdomen. You'll be able to do this through your hands that are folded on top of your navel. When you are doing this correctly, you'll know when you see your belly expanding as you breathe in and drawing back inwards as you exhale.

6. If this is your first time doing breathwork, don't be discouraged if you're not able to get this right the first time. The important thing is to practice this consistently, and over time, you'll be able to learn how to breathe like a baby, i.e., barely breathe properly and do it naturally.

Another way you can tell you have learned to do this properly and naturally if it feels like your lungs are gently massaging your belly organs. Also, rejuvenation, feeling centered, and being relaxed are other ways to confirm that you're doing it right. Don't overstrain, and when you feel it's becoming uncomfortable, you may need to adjust accordingly.

Kidney Breathing

In the medical application of Qigong, physiology and energy are determined by specific internal organs. The lungs are primarily responsible for getting energy from the air. But the kidneys are primarily responsible for pulling the air energy in your lungs to bring it even deeper to the rest of your body. You may think of your kidneys as rechargeable batteries, which is where you can store air energy for future use, but just like physical batteries, they also get depleted over time. Through kidney breathing, you'll be able to recharge those batteries, massage your kidneys, and make your diaphragm stronger at the same time. If you forgot, the kidneys are positioned in your lower back area, with each kidney on one side of your spine. On top of them, you'll find your adrenal glands.

Kidney breathing is done best while standing up, ideally after performing the original breath exercise. Here's how to do it:

1. Stand with both feet parallel to each other and about shoulder-width apart. Just like the original breath, you must also keep your knees slightly bent and soft. Make sure that your knees never go ahead of your toes.

2. Now, place your hands on your lower back with your palms holding your lower back just above your hips and the fingers pointing downward toward your spine and sacrum.

3. Next, tuck your tailbone beneath your torso. An easy way to do this is by imitating a monkey trying to move its tail forward between its legs. By doing this, you'll be able to naturally straighten out your lower spine's natural curve.

4. Similar to how you expand your belly in the original breath, use your hands to feel your lower back expand. Unlike the movement in your belly, it'll be more subtle.

5. As you breathe out, use your hands to feel your lower back to contract or relax.

6. As you breathe in this position, start to slightly tilt your hips with every breath. While breathing in, tuck your tailbone beneath your body to curve your lower back slightly like how a monkey moves its tail forward beneath its legs.

7. As you exhale, resume your lower spine's natural curve by untucking your tailbone or bringing the monkey tail back. As you do this, be careful to do this slowly, softly, and smoothly to minimize your risks for spinal disc injuries, especially if you have a history of it.

8. To enhance your lower back's movement, you can slightly constrict or tense your abdominal muscles. By doing this, you won't be able to expand your belly as you breathe, but instead, it will be redirected to your lower back or the kidney area.

9. As your diaphragm and lungs are pushed downward and back, your adrenal glands and kidneys can enjoy a good massage and, in the process, improve both blood cleansing and hormonal activities.

Kidney breathing can be a bit challenging to perform, especially initially. However, it will help you strengthen your diaphragm in the long run. Ultimately, this can help you make breathing more natural and much easier. If you have lower back pain, this exercise can be therapeutic and provide adequate support for your lumbar spine.

Cleansing Breath

The third Qigong breathing exercise is, as the name implies, one that helps you energize and clean your body. In the process, it will also help you achieve a calm mind. If you've ever felt stressed, tired, or lethargic in the middle of the afternoon, the cleansing breath exercise can help you feel rejuvenated and relaxed. It is not only easy to learn, but it only takes up to 10 minutes every day to practice or as short as needed to give you an energy boost in the afternoon. Here's how to do it:

1. Look for a quiet place where you can practice the cleansing breath in a relaxed manner without being disturbed. Ideally, do it sitting on a chair that allows you to have good posture with your neck and back straight and with both your feet flat on the floor. During the exercise, don't cross your legs or feet.

2. Next, put your hands on top of your lap in a folded position with the right one on top of the left. If you prefer, you may place them on your knees separately instead.

3. Let the tip of your tongue touch your palate, i.e., the roof of your mouth just at the back of your upper teeth. Keep it there for the rest of the exercise.

4. Take deep breaths and relax your body before proceeding with the exercise.

5. Just like with the original breath, this exercise involves deep belly breathing, where you expand your belly instead of your chest when you inhale and let your belly draw back in as you breathe out. With each belly breath, you're able to fill your lungs with air up to its full capacity. Every time you exhale, ensure that you get as much air out of your lungs as possible.

6. Start the exercise by breathing slowly through your mouth. During the exhale, picture in your mind's eye dark-colored toxins and carbon dioxide departing from every part of your body.

7. On the next breath, do it slowly through your nose and visualize healing white energy and oxygen being distributed to and absorbed by all parts of your body. As it does so, your entire body is cleansed and nourished.

8. Hold the breath and as you do, continue visualizing the white energy and oxygen nourishing and cleansing your entire body. Then, exhale as much air from your lungs, also visualizing dark-colored toxins and carbon dioxide exiting your body.

9. Repeat the entire process for about 5 to 10 minutes every day.

How long should you hold your breath, and how many seconds should each inhale and exhale require? The ideal counts are 2-1-4, i.e., exhale in multiple counts of two seconds, inhale in multiple counts of 1 second, and hold your breath for multiple counts of four seconds. If it's too much to process initially, start using the box breathing technique. This means inhaling, holding the breath exactly, and holding the exhale position for the same length of time, e.g., 5-5-5-5 or 4-4-4-4. Again, the key here is that you shouldn't feel strained with the duration. Increase it over time, without too much strain.

Breathing this way can help improve blood and oxygen circulation to your brain and other body parts of your body. It will also help promote relaxation and optimal flow of qi in your meridians and organs. Over time, practicing the cleansing breath regularly can help you achieve a calmer mind and greatly reduce your life stress.

Reverse Breathing, Daoist Style

Compared to the first three, this one can be a bit more challenging to perform. Its primary goal is to intensify the meridian flow and purify the body. As such, it is a very good breathing exercise when performing Qigong movements or meditating.

The best way to master this breathing style is by learning how to breathe properly first. In particular, you must learn yogic breathing first. When you're able to do that, you can start on the Daoist reverse breathing technique. Here's how to perform this technique:

1. Sit down with your shoulders, neck, and head relaxed.

2. Touch your palate or the roof of your mouth using the tip of your tongue.

3. Keep your spine straight and long.

4. Put both hands on your lower abdomen with the right hand on top of the left one.

5. Breathe in through your chest, letting your ribs expand. When this happens, let your lower abdomen contract.

6. Allow your lower abdomen, just below your navel, to pull closer to your spine. When this happens, you should be able to feel it move away from your hands in a gentle and scooping manner. This helps your qi flow up your spine.

7. When you breathe out, allow your belly to resume its original position.

8. Perform this breathing movement ten times.

While this type of breathing can be more challenging to learn than the first three, it will be a great breathing technique for meditating or doing Qigong. Don't be impatient. Take your time learning this breathing technique because it'll be worth doing right.

When you combine this with a movement-based practice like Qigong, it's important to coordinate both. Ideally, do this by exhaling as you move your body and inhaling while holding a position.

Box-Breathing

Of all the breathing techniques thought in this chapter, this is probably the simplest and easiest to perform. This technique was popularized by former US Navy Seal and best-selling author Mark Divine in his popular book "Unbeatable Mind." It's called box breathing because all four phases of this exercise, i.e., the inhale, holding the inhale, exhale, and holding the exhale, all require the same length of time. Breathe through the nose only.

Divine recommends five seconds for each phase, but if it's too long for you, you can start with something shorter and gradually lengthened the periods. Initially, go for at least five minutes per session. Gradually increase the duration over time.

This is also a very practical way to relax and calm yourself down when you're feeling highly stressed or anxious. After a few breathing cycles, you'll notice your heart rate slowing down to help you relax.

Prepare for the Breathing Exercises

To get the most out of your Qigong breathing sessions, there are things you can do beforehand. Some include:

1. Putting yourself in the right mental state, i.e., one that's relaxed and not in a hurry.

2. Settling yourself in a place that is quiet and distraction-free.

3. Block off time from your schedule to ensure the consistent practice of these techniques. Consistency is key for experiencing the benefits of these breathing exercises.

4. Wear comfortable fitting clothes to ensure free-flowing qi. Tight clothes hinder deep breathing and can constrict the flow of your qi.

Chapter 6: The Dantian: Activating Core Energy

What is the Dantian? In traditional Chinese medicine, this is frequently called the stored *energy center* for the body. It's also worth noting that a Dantian isn't the same as a chakra. The latter is an energy gateway, while the Dantian is an energy storage center.

The Three Dantians

Each of the three is closely linked to specific elements: fire, water, and earth. These are the lower, middle, and upper Dantians.

The Lower Dantian

You can find this in your lower abdomen area, about three fingers below your navel and two fingers behind it. This Dantian is responsible for creating your essence or jing energy. Traditional Chinese medicine considers the lowered Dantian as the "superior ultimate" of all the Qigong treasures.

It is also called the golden stove. In ancient Chinese culture, the lower Dantian is believed to be the foundation for several important aspects of martial arts and Qigong-like balancing, breathing, rooted standing, and awareness of one's entire body. Many also call it the roots of the tree of life and where a person's internal energy or qi comes from, common in the Chinese, Japanese, and Korean cultures.

Many of those who teach Buddhism and Taoism instruct their followers to prioritize their Dantian because it allows them to learn of the universe's greater mind. Ultimately, it helps activate their higher state of consciousness or samadhi.

One reason this Dantian is believed to be the most important of the three treasures it's because of its position. Unless it's activated and opened, you won't be able to sense or feel you're two other Dantians, i.e., the upper and middle ones. When it's blocked or closed, which is the case for most people, you won't be able to tap into your renewable energy. Instead, you must get energy mainly from sources that are not renewable both inside your body and in your environment. This tends to deplete not just your internal resources but your environmental ones as well.

But if you're able to activate and keep this gateway open, you'll be evil to enjoy abundant energy directly from its source. This energy type can also flow freely through your chakras and meridians, so every muscle, organ, and body part is energized. Along the way, thoroughly energizing every part of your body can help you relax and feel more confident, too.

This type of energy also helps clear your channels of the negative energies absorbed by your body's cells throughout the years. Some also call this the *cellular purification process.*

When you have successfully activated your lower Dantian, this cleansing energy you can freely travel from your body's center up through your chakra system. Along the way, it clears your energy pathways such that qi can freely flow and nourish every cell in your body. Ultimately, it keeps pushing upward until it arrives at the top of your head, where it generates highly positive emotions and illuminates your entire body, mind, and spirit.

As you do this, you'll be able to reconnect to a state of love and openness often called enlightenment or samadhi. This includes a process of being born, receiving global and ancestral karma, experiencing sufferings, dying a thousand deaths, the ability to establish a divine connection, divine transformation, and to experience the entire human transformation journey.

You may also think of these as the source and rise of kundalini energy. Particularly in Hindu culture, kundalini is believed to be strong divine energy that resembles a coiled snake at the root chakra or base of a person's spine. Viewed as a divine feminine power or shakti energy, kundalini energy is created primarily through methods like pranayama breathing, meditation, mantra chanting, tantra, and asana practice.

Many practitioners look at the Taoist and Hindu energy concepts as being slightly different in terms of what they do but basically have the same source. You may think of your lower Dantian as the creator or manufacturer of your vital life energy and the kundalini you awaken as the fuel that powers the creator or generator.

Middle Dantian

This one is positioned at your heart level, and it's the center of power for your emotions and thoughts. The middle Dantian is linked to your internal organs' health (particularly your thymus gland) and the respiratory system. Called the crimson palace, your middle Dantian produces vital energy or qi, which is your air energy or, in a figurative sense, your life force.

The heart is the power center of love, from which all things are created. It's the only healing force in the world, and as such, it's important for achieving optimal health and well-being.

Many people feel unloved simply because their middle Dantian has yet to open fully. If you don't feel as loved despite knowing in your mind that people do love you, your middle Dantian probably isn't fully opened yet. As you learn to activate and open this one up, you'll be able to feel an increasing amount of love in your life.

If that were the case, you might be wondering why you are unconsciously keeping your lower Dantian from fully opening up? Because the lower Dantian tends to push powerful energy up to your heart that manifests itself as love. When this happens, you may awaken your kundalini energy, which can lead to a surge of emotions, leading to the cleansing of emotional pain. Because this can feel unpleasant or painful, the natural tendency is to avoid it altogether, and thus, it's probably the reason you and many other people keep your lowered Dantian from fully opening up. However, the pain or discomfort is necessary to allow the kundalini or qi energy to cleanse and clear your meridian paths and facilitate optimal flow to the upper Dantian and crown chakra, also known as *Sahasrara*.

Your lower Dantian has the power to amplify the love you receive and give to others. When you can properly develop or activate your middle Dantian, you can ensure that the positive force coming from the lower one can reach the upper one. When this happens, the potential for optimal health and well-being is maximized.

Upper Dantian

The last of the three Dantians is positioned between and above your eyebrows. This is commonly referred to in Hindu culture as the *ajna chakra* or the third eye. The organ that is most associated with this specific power center is the pineal gland. The spirit or consciousness is the primary area of concern of the upper Dantian.

Others also called this Dantian a muddy pellet and believe this power center is the one that creates the shen energy in Chinese culture. Here, once spirit or shen is further refined into pure consciousness.

When your vital life forces can reach this power center, your brain can experience a huge burst of energy that can permeate every energetic and biological system in your body. As this happens, a powerful light floods these systems, silencing your ego or conscious mind. In turn, more divine intelligence is available for your brain to perform a vast number of complex functions. It allows you to achieve optimal cognitive performance and the sense of being one with the universe.

Synthetically, this same level of consciousness can also be awakened through psychoactive drugs like MDMA, certain types of mushrooms, DMT, and other psychoactive plants like ayahuasca. However, these are unnatural ways of doing so, and because they can rapidly bring people to such a level of consciousness, they may not be ready for the experience.

But with Qigong, you can gradually achieve such a level of consciousness at a pace comfortable for you. As such, your experience will be more beneficial than traumatic or super intense.

Dantian Weaknesses

Your Dantians are crucial for optimal health and well-being within your practice of Qigong. That is why you must also be familiar with signs that tell you when getting weak.

For example, your vital energy can float upward when it's not focused on your lower Dantian. When this happens, you risk disturbing your upper Dantian. This may negatively affect you emotionally and mentally, making minor nuisances and issues feel worse and bigger than they really are.

If left unchecked, it may cause you to lose sight of your life's essence and purpose, leading to an unfulfilled life. Unresolved, these may eventually lead to disease and distress.

When your lower Dantian performs poorly, you must get more energy from your prenatal qi reserves every day. Considering this is a finite resource, you won't be able to sustain this practice in the long run. When your lower Dantian is functioning optimally, it's like you're running on solar, wind, or nuclear energy - all of which are renewable. Otherwise, it's like trying to run on fossil fuel or coal that is limited in quantities.

When your middle Dantian is closed, it will be challenging for you to connect with your emotions or your heart. As a result, it will feel like you're not receiving enough love in your life despite the contrary. It will also affect your ability to love other people, and you'll likely feel uninspired, unmotivated, and disconnected from others.

Finally, it is very hard to look forward to the future when your upper Dantian is not performing well. Some ways you can tell this is happening are when you feel lacking in vitality or when people tell you you've lost the sparkle in your eyes.

This isn't something to be taken lightly because often, the way we live our lives is primarily influenced by this area. We risk living a life devoid of purpose and fulfillment ask there will be a disconnection from the two other Dantians, i.e., the heart and the essence. The best way to live life is through synergistic cooperation between the lower, middle, and upper Dantians.

Strengthening Your Dantian

So, what can you do to strengthen your Dantian when it's weak?

Given that it's the most important of the three treasures, it is important to ground and strengthen your lower Dantian first. If you do this, the two other Dantians will also benefit from it. This doesn't mean working on your lower Dantian is all that's needed to strengthen the whole. You'll still need to strengthen the two other Dantians, but if you focus on the lower part first, it can be much easier to improve the others.

How do you strengthen your lower Dantian? While acupuncture treatment is the best way to do it, practicing lower Dantian breathing allows the treatment to optimize the Dantian strengthening results.

Lower Dantian strengthening exercises allow you to better hold and build your qi. It also gives you a stronger core, which improves your body's stability and lowers your risk of falling off balance and getting injured. Through lower Dantian breathing, you can be happier, less stressed, and healthier.

Here's a simple meditative lower Dantian breathing exercise you can do regularly for strengthening said area:

1. Assume and hold an erect posture.

2. Keep your feet parallel to each other and about shoulder-width apart.

3. Keep your knees slightly bent and soft, so the joints don't bear the entire weight.

4. Pull your pelvis forward while keeping your spine straight.

5. Keep your head straight with your neck pulled back.

6. Think of a string passing through your head down to your spine all the way to the ground between your feet.

7. Take a deep breath and bring it down all the way to your lower Dantian through the imaginary string.

8. When you inhale, expand your lower abdomen as your diaphragm expands, too.

9. Then, visualize a warm ball of energy in your lower Dantian area, which is about five fingers below your navel and three fingers behind it.

10. Every time you inhale, imagine the energy ball growing.

11. As you exhale, see the same ball shrinking.

12. Do this a couple of times, and afterward, put your palms on top of your lower Dantian and continue the breathing

exercise. Doing so can help you become conscious of your Dantian during the exercise.

13. If you're a man, your right hand should be on top of the left one. If you're a woman, the left should be on top of the right.

14. Practice this exercise for 10 to 15 minutes every day and gradually increase the duration over time at a comfortable pace.

You may also strengthen your lower Dantian through mindful movements such as aikido or tai chi. In these martial arts, the primary focus is on your lower Dantian. By focusing on this, you become more grounded and stable physically.

After strengthening your lower Dantian, it's time to focus on the upper one. Here's a practical exercise to help you do that.

1. Start by focusing your attention on the crown of your head. Imagine an 8-shaped figure on top of it lying horizontally across your scalp. Choose any point on the surface of the imaginary 8-shaped figure. Imagine there's a pen fixed on that position. Slowly "draw" an 8-shaped figure on your crown by moving your head instead of the "pencil."

2. Coordinate this movement with your breathing to activate your cranial pump. To do this, imagine your cranial plates being pulled apart to widen their seams as you exhale. As you inhale, imagine the opposite act, i.e., your cranial blades being pulled together with its seams narrowing.

3. Repeat steps one and two at least eight times.

4. Next, visualize the eight-shaped figure going down into your brain and, as it does, see it transform into a Mobius strip, which is an 8-shaped figure with no intersecting points.

5. Imagine a thread by visually tracing a line that runs across your brain that ghost near the corpus callosum, which resides between your brain's two hemispheres.

6. When you practice this exercise regularly, you'll be able to achieve greater harmony between your right and left brain. This can help you combine your creative and analytical thinking skills, which are your right and left brain's key functions, respectively.

7. At certain times, slow things down and create a long "nnnnnnnn" sound with your tongue touching your pallet and your mouth half-closed. You can direct the sound waves produced towards your cranial vault. In turn, this can conduct the vibratory response in the middle of your brain, where traditional bridges and gateways to the spiritual plane are located, such as the pineal and pituitary glands, the thalamus, and the hypothalamus.

8. When you're done, express gratitude and smile your left and right brain.

Strengthening your Dantian can take time. Hence, be patient and continue regularly practicing at a pace comfortable for you. It will come, I assure you.

Chapter 7: Practical Qigong: Warm-Ups

Before practicing Qigong movements, remember this - despite how gentle and flowing the movements are, you should still warm up before proceeding. Here are some excellent warm-up movements to prepare for your Qigong sessions.

1. Finger stretches: start by putting the palm of your hand down on a flat surface or a table. Gently, make your fingers as straight as possible against it without forcing or putting a strain on your joints. Hold it's for 30 to 60 seconds before releasing and repeat at least four times.

2. Wrist rotations: clasp both hands and perform several rotations, starting with a clockwise movement followed by a counterclockwise one.

3. Elbow rotations: bring your arms up to your sides to form a big cross with your body. While keeping your upper arms (biceps and triceps) steady, move your forearms in a circular motion several times. Start with a forward motion followed by a backward motion.

4. Shoulder rotations: rotate each of your upper arms at shoulder level several times, starting with the forward movement followed by a backward one. To have an idea of how to do this properly, imagine drawing large circles on each side of your body using your elbows.

5. Waist rotations: move your hips sideward, forward, to the other side, and backward in a smooth and circular flow. Perform several repetitions for each direction.

6. Knee rotations: stand with both feet close together and slightly bent and both hands resting on top of your knees. In a smooth circular motion, move your knees to one side, forward, through the other side, to the back, and back to the side for several repetitions. Then, do them again for the same number of reps flowing in the opposite direction this time.

7. Ankle rotations: start by planting the toes of one of your feet on the ground and use it as the base on which you'll rotate your ankle for several repetitions in one direction before reversing the movement for the same number of reps. Do the same for the other foot.

8. Spine rotations: stand with your feet parallel to each other and about shoulder width, with one arm raised forward and the other up your back. Look at your backhand by turning your head, then swing your arms down by your sights and up again to switch hand positions. Imagine doing a running man position with your arm switching positions while running. When forward raised arm goes to the back, turn your head so you can look at it. This creates a gentle twist in your spine. Repeat this movement several times smoothly and rhythmically.

Chapter 8: Practical Qigong: Essential Exercises

Each exercise is closely related to a specific organ in your body, each having its specific peak activity periods within the day/night. These are arranged in chronological order based on their related organ's peak activity, starting with the gall bladder that peaks between 11:00 pm and 1:00 am.

To get the most out of your daily Qigong routine, start it by performing the exercise whose related organ's peak activity coincides with the time of your practice. For example, start with the Body Bend & Head Swing exercise if you plan to do Qigong between 5:00 am and 7:00 am. Then, just follow the sequence of the exercises below to end with the exercise before the one you started with. In this example, you'll end the session with the Path-Clearing Dragon. Adjust accordingly based on the time you'll work out.

Again, prioritize proper form. You need not perform all the exercises at once. Learn one or two, and once you've mastered them, add another one until you've mastered all the 12 exercises.

The Tiger's Back Stretch

This exercise is closely related to your gallbladder, and its peak activity is between 11:00 pm to 1:00 am. Here's how to perform the exercise:

1. Start by assuming the bow stance. Your hands should be in front of you, with the right one held high in the left one held low.

2. Turn your body to the left and as you do so, breathe in.

3. Lower your stance and extend both arms forward while exhaling.

4. Bring your hands up above your head as you continue to exhale. Let your gaze follow your hands.

5. Finish the move by looking behind you.

6. Return to your original position by turning right and as you do, inhale.

7. Repeat the movement by turning in the opposite direction, i.e., turning your body to the right with your left hand held high and your right one held low.

The Four Body Movements

This exercise is related to your liver, whose peak activity is from 1:00 am to 3:00 am. Here are the steps:

1. Begin by assuming the bow stance.

2. Turn to your left side and assume a lunging position. Exhale as you do this.

3. As you perform a lunge, make sure that your knees never go beyond your toes to prevent knee strain.

4. Lunge backward (to the right while still facing left) to shift your weight to your right leg. Inhale as you do this and make sure your knee never goes beyond the toes.

5. While maintaining this position, bend at the waist to lean your upper body towards your left leg. Keep your lower back as straight as possible to minimize risks for strain and injuries. Make sure your pelvis is over your right leg throughout the movement, too.

6. Go back to the forward lunging position to shift your body weight to your left leg again. Exhale as you do this and make sure the left knee never goes beyond the toes.

7. Continue exhaling as you turn to the right to return to the original or starting bow stance. Repeat this in the opposite direction.

The Path-Clearing Dragon

This exercise is related to your lungs, whose speak activity is between 3:00 a.m. and 5:00 a.m. Here are the steps to performing it:

1. Begin by standing in a horse stance.

2. Clench your fists and draw back your elbows so they are directly in line with your waist.

3. Turn to your left side, ending in a bow stance.

4. Exhale as you bring out your left fist in front of you from your center, as if you're punching somebody but in a very slow manner. Stop short of locking your elbows.

5. Bring up your extended left arm in a circular manner to bring your fist behind you. Inhale as you do this and keep your gaze on your fist.

6. Reverse the motion to bring your fist back directly above your head and continue breathing in as you do this.

7. Bring your fist back in front of your body, with the arm remaining extended. Exhale as you do this.

8. Cap off the movement by bringing your fist back in line with your waist to resume the starting position. Inhale as you do this.

9. Repeat this sequence facing the other direction and using your right arm.

Body Bend & Head Swing

This exercise involves your large intestine, whose peak activity is between 5:00 am to 7:00 am. Follow these steps to perform it properly:

1. Start by assuming a low horse stance and rest both hands on top of your knees so you can use your arms to support your body weight and avoid straining your lower back throughout the movement.

2. Use your upper body to draw a circle. Do this by bringing down your body towards the left, to the center, then bring it back up to the right side before returning to your original horse stance position. Try to make the biggest circle you can with your head. Inhale throughout this movement.

3. Repeat this to complete one sequence, going the other direction and exhaling throughout the movement.

4. Repeat the sequence. This time, inhale while going to the right and exhale as you go left.

The One-Arm Raise

This exercise involves your stomach, which reaches peak activity between 7:00 am to 9:00 am. Here are the steps:

1. Start by standing with your feet close together.

2. In front of your naval, bring your palms together with the left one on top of your right.

3. Bring your left hand up and the right hand down simultaneously while tiptoeing, breathing out while doing these.

4. Make a large circle with your hands, ending with your right hand up high and your left hand down low. Breathe in as you do this.

5. As you resume a flat-footed position, bring your palms close together with the right hand over the left this time. Continue inhaling as you do this.

6. Repeat the movement, this time in the other direction. Put your right palm over your left palm, then circle your hands in the opposite direction. As you perform this movement, inhale, then exhale as you return to the starting position.

The Hind-Looking Crane

The exercise involves your spleen, with activity peaking between 9:00 is to 11:00 am. Perform this exercise through these steps:

1. Start by assuming the ma bu or horse stance. Raise both arms to the sides up to shoulder level, inhaling as you do this.

2. Lower your arms to your sides and face your left side. Bring your right arm up forward and your left one backward. As you do this, turn both feet such that each forms a 45-degree angle facing outward, i.e., the left foot forms a 45-degree angle to the left while the right one forms a 45-degree angle to the right. Continue inhaling as you do these.

3. Do the same movement but this time, turning towards your right side. Exhale as you do this to complete one sequence.

4. Repeat the whole sequence. This time, breathe in while turning to your right, then breathe out as you turn to your left.

The Wing-Beating Wild Goose

The organ related to this exercise is your heart, whose peak activity is between 11:00 am to 1:00 pm. Here's how correctly performed the exercise:

1. Start by assuming a horse stance.

2. Clench your fists and bring your elbows back such that your fists are in line with your body. Inhale as you do this.

3. Raise your fists upward over your head touch your nape, keeping your elbows bent. In the process, you are raising your elbows above and slightly in front of your head. Exhale as you do this.

4. Reverse the movement and bring your elbows back to their original position, then rolling them up and forward in a circular motion. The circular movement of your elbows by pointing them directly forward. Continue breathing out while doing this.

5. Straighten your arms to extend them forward. Extend your fingers as well while continuing to exhale.

6. Go back to your starting position by bringing back your fists beside your waist. Breathe in as you do.

Wind-Punching

This exercise is linked to your small intestine, whose peak activity is between 1:00 pm to 3:00 pm. Here are the steps to performing it:

1. Begin by assuming a horse stance with your elbows drawn back so your fists are in line with your waist. Breathe in ask you do the latter.

2. Extend your left arm and bring your left fist forward as if punching something in front of you slowly and steadily while breathing out. Don't lock your arms but instead, stop short of locking your elbows instead.

3. While keeping your upper arm and elbow fixed pointing forward, draw a circle with your left fist by swinging it down toward your center, then up and forward in front of you, with your left arm extended forward and back to the punch position. Continue exhaling.

4. Next, turn your hand over and stretch your fingers while continuing to breathe out.

5. To conclude the movement, return your left fist to its original position beside your waist. Inhale as you do this.

6. Perform the same movement with the other arm.

The Black Tiger Straight Waist

This exercise is closely linked to your bladder, and its activity peaks between 3:00 pm to 5:00 pm kick it. Here are the steps to perform this:

1. Stand straight with your feet about shoulder-width apart and arms to the sides. Keep your knees slightly bent.

2. Bend forward at the waist and interlock your fingers as you inhale. Keep your lower back straight throughout the movement to minimize risks for lower back strain or injuries.

3. Return to your standing position and raise your arms up and forward to shoulder level. Breathe out as you do this and keep your fingers locked.

4. Bring down your arms and pull them back as far as you can while breathing in.

5. Reverse the movement by swinging them forward, up, and backward past your head. At this point, you're back should be slightly arched backward. Exhale as you perform this movement.

6. Reverse the movement and bring down your arms while continuing to exhale.

7. Raise your arms forward, up, and back over your head again while continuing to exhale.

8. As you bring them down again, do your sides, breathe in.

The Horse-Riding Archer

In this exercise, you'll be working your kidneys, which reach their peak activity between 5:00 pm to 7:00 pm. Here are the steps:

1. Start by assuming the horse stance with your arms to the sides.

2. Turn your head to your left. Bring your arms up such that your left hand is in front of your left shoulder with its left finger stretched, and your right hand is just behind it with all fingers extended. Inhale while doing these.

3. Extend your left arm to your left side and think of your index finger as a bow by which you will launch arrows later. Bring back your right hand to the center of your chest or in front of your right nipple as if you were pulling back the bow's string to launch an arrow. As you do these, breathe out.

4. Bring your arms down back to your sides and inhale while doing so.

5. Perform the same movements, this time facing your right side and with opposite arms and hands.

Turn & Gaze

The second to the last exercise is closely linked to your pericardium or circulation sex organ. Its peak activity lies between 7:00 pm and 9:00 pm, and here's how to practice the exercise:

1. Begin by assuming a horse stance with arms to your sides.

2. Circle both hands such that the right hand is at the bottom of the circle while the left one is on top. As you form the circle, breathe in.

3. Bring your hands to close together and continue inhaling while doing so.

4. Press both hands forward with your right-hand low and the left-hand high. Exhale while doing this.

5. Twist your body to the left, keeping your eyes fixed on your left hand and continuing to exhale as you do.

6. Reverse the movement and twist to your right side, still fixing your eyes on the left hand while breathing out.

7. Return to the middle and face forwards while inhaling.

8. Create a circle using your hands again. This time bring your right hand to the top of the circle and your left hand to the bottom. Continue inhaling.

9. Bring your palms together in front of your body as you continue breathing in.

10. Repeat steps 1 to 9 but this time, exhaling while you bring your hands forward with your right hand above and your left hand below. Continue exhaling while twisting your body to the right and then to the left.

Hands Pushing the Sky

This exercise involves your triple warmer organ, the peak activity of which is from 9:00 pm to 11:00 pm. Here are the steps:

1. Stand up straight with your feet about shoulder-width apart and your hands to your sides.

2. Next, raise both arms to your sides until they are at shoulder height or parallel to the ground. Breathe in when you do this movement.

3. Bring your hands on top of your head and interlock your fingers while continuing to breathe in.

4. Turn your palms downside up.

5. While keeping your fingers interlocked, push your hands upward and extend your arms while exhaling. Simultaneously, raise your body up by tiptoeing and look upward.

6. Bring your hands back down to the top of your head, still breathing out.

7. Turn your palms upside down, with fingers still interlocked, so your palms are touching the top of your head.

8. Unlock your fingers, straighten your arms, and lower them down back to shoulder level or until parallel to the ground. Breathe in while doing this.

9. At this position, rotate your palms so they are now facing the floor.

Complete the sequence by bringing your arms down back to your sides, exhaling as you do so.

Chapter 9: The Qi Diet

There is a saying: we are what we eat. Our general health and wellbeing depend largely on the quality of our diet. We can optimize health and wellbeing with a healthy diet and vice versa.

Qigong is primarily known for its movements, postures, and breathing, but it's also influenced by nutrition. Remember that our qi or internal life force energy is also affected by what we put inside our bodies. These include the air we breathe and the food we eat.

At the most basic level, the human body gets its energy in the form of calories from the foods consumed. More than just delivering essential caloric energy, they also provide our body's cells with elemental energies, which can also affect our mind and spirit. Hence, what we eat is crucial for optimizing the benefits of Qigong.

Individualized

One of the more important characteristics of a Qigong-aligned diet is individualization. Simply put, this means an optimal diet is most likely different from one person to another, both in terms of quantity and quality of food.

Given this, how would you know the best foods for your health and wellbeing as part of the Qigong practice? Honestly, there is no one best answer to that question because there is really not one best diet that applies to everybody. You are a unique person as much as everybody else differs from one another, and what may constitute the best Qigong diet for you may differ from what constitutes the same for me and everybody else. To that extent, you must pay close attention to your body and how certain foods affect how you feel and how you perform.

Luckily, you need not labor over studying different types of food and their potential impact on your body because the human body itself is wise enough to know what foods are good and bad for it. Learn how to pay close attention to your body because it will help you discover which foods to focus on and what to avoid.

You also need to be honest with yourself about how specific types of food affect you after meals. Sometimes, we tend to justify our favorite food and drinks, even if they make us feel terrible after eating them. If you acknowledge their true effects on you, it'll be easier for you to eat optimally and experience Qigong's benefits.

There are certain foods whose post-meal effects are very glaring and obvious. Some of these post-eating impacts include nausea, pain in the tummy, or even fatigue. When the effects are very clear, there's no need for a careful evaluation.

But there are certain foods whose negative impacts aren't as obvious because they are so subtle. That is why unless you observe very obvious side effects, take the time to sit down with yourself and thoroughly check your energy levels and how you feel.

As you make this a habit, you'll develop the ability to easily notice have different types of food and drinks impact you afterward regardless of how subtle the effects may be. As Qigong is based on a subtle form of energy, the same goes for your diet.

When you're too busy with so many things or when you're running on autopilot, i.e., lack of mindfulness, it's very easy to ignore your qi. If you practice mindfulness in your life, you'll be able to slow things down enough to feel the changes in your qi and in other areas of your life, including nutrition, among others.

Food, the Elements, and Seasons

An important element or principle for eating for optimal health and wellbeing when it comes to Qigong is the relationship of food to specific elements and seasons.

With our dietary requirements, most of it is determined by our body's composition. Based on traditional Chinese medicine, a person comprises energy elements, or the five basic elements - earth, fire, wood, water, and metal.

While it's true that we all belong to the same ecosystem called nature, and our bodies are made of the same "materials," one way each of us differs from the other is the ratio and proportion or amount of each element. Just as modern science teaches that each person comprises a unique DNA code, traditional Chinese medicine uses the concept of the five elements to convey the same.

Based on this concept, you require specific types of foods and specific amounts, in ways different from everyone else's, based on the relative amounts and proportions of the five elements inside your body. Every type of food and taste has different effects on your elemental energies.

Take, for example, the fire element. It's probably obvious to you that this refers to the foods that are warm and spicy. How about the water element? It pertains to foods that are cooling and salty. Foods related to the wood element are warm and sour. Foods related to the metal element are generally pungent and mildly cooling. Foods related to the earth are neutral in temperature and tend to be sweet.

Here's a summary of each element's relationship to specific types of food and the particular organs involved:

1. Earth, yellowish and sweet foods, and the organs involved are the spleen and stomach.

2. Metal, white-colored spicy/acrid foods, and the organs involved are large intestines and lungs.

3. Water, blue/black-colored salty foods, and the organs involved are the bladder and kidneys.

4. Wood, green-colored sour foods, and the organs involved are the gallbladder and liver.

5. Fire, red-colored spicy or bitter food, and the organs involved are the small intestines and the heart.

After reading this, you'll be able to easily figure out how all these come together, especially if you're familiar with how the organs in your body work. Just like with other areas of Qigong, the relationship of the five elements with food and organs aren't arbitrary; but instead, they are based on sound principles and are linked to actual physical properties both of your body and your environment.

Foods that have yellowish color contain higher amounts of specific types of nutrients in as much as the other colored foods also contain higher amounts of specific types of nutrients.

More than just their colors, specific flavors also affect your body in different ways. For example, think about how your body reacts when you eat or bite a slice of lemon as compared to when you drink soda. The slice of lemon makes your mouth produce a lot of saliva, while the cold soda helps you feel refreshed and cool.

Such physical reactions aren't just limited to superficial ones. Similar reactions can happen with specific organs in the body responsible for digesting, absorbing, and using the nutrients.

How can you apply this information between the relationship of food, elemental energies, and organs to your Qigong diet? A few ways include:

1. Eat more sour food to activate your liver more.

2. Eat better foods to make your small intestines and heart more robust.

3. To achieve better activity balance among your organs, include a little of each type of flavor every time you eat.

4. To enjoy more nutrient-balanced meals, consider eating foods with a wide variety of colors per sitting.

More than just the elements, a diet optimized for Qigong's benefits consider the seasons. More than just affecting the environment you live in, seasons can also play a role in who you are as a person and your specific needs.

One very obvious example is alcohol. There's a reason why strong liquors tend to be very popular in countries with very cold weather: they help raise body temperature. Another example is cold lemonade. While very popular during the hot summer season, it's hardly in demand during the rainy and cold winter months.

Your body knows what it needs to achieve equilibrium during specific seasons. Hence, cravings for certain types of food and drinks according to the general climate and weather. During cold seasons, your body craves hot or heat-inducing food and drinks, while during hot and humid seasons, it craves for food and drinks that are cold.

Eating Habits

It's not just what you eat and drink that determines your health and wellbeing. How you eat has a big say, too. It's because food and drinks don't just contain nutrients but also, to some extent, emotions. That's why you're eating habits mustn't be just optimal for giving your physical body nourishment but emotional ones too.

You may be wondering, how do you "consume" or get enough nourishing emotions? One way is to take your time eating and not to hurry up your meals. While it's true that we live in a fast-paced society, it doesn't mean eating fast and mindlessly to rush to the next task is the best way to get needed calories. In fact, eating food in a very hurried manner and with little to no mindfulness increases the likelihood of you eating foods void of nourishing calories and eating more than what's needed.

But more than these, eating at a hurried and stressful pace can also make you feel more anxious and mentally and emotionally stressed. The point of eating is to replenish the body's nutrients and restore its vitality. Eating this way isn't just counterproductive - it's unhealthy, too. When you slow down your eating, you treat every meal as a sacred space to restore and rejuvenate your mind, body, and spirit.

What does eating mindfully actually mean? One of the most practical or objective ways of doing it is by chewing your food a minimum number of times with every bite. The ancient Taoist recommendation is at least 50 times. Considering this is too much for most people, you can go for 20 to 30 bites instead.

Why should you chew your food many times before swallowing every bite? It's because digestion doesn't start in the stomach - but *in the mouth*. Chewing food many times helps break it down substantially, and together with your saliva, it preps the food for optimal digestion and extraction of nutrients in the stomach once you swallow them. Therefore, taking your time to chew your food as long as possible can help your body get as many nutrients as it can from food. Doing so also helps you savor the taste for as long as possible, making mealtime even more joyful.

Another important eating habit to develop about a Qigong-friendly diet is never to drink cold beverages during meals. Why? Doing so increases the risk of quenching; they just in fires in your stomach. Instead, bear your meals with warm liquids to help optimize digestion in your stomach and allow your body to get the most nutrients out of every meal. It's best to drink cold or cool beverages outside of meals.

While this list isn't all-encompassing for mindful eating practices and optimal nourishment, it's a great place to start.

Yin, Yang, and Your Food

Food can also be characterized based on the principles of yin and yang. To be more specific, we were talking about the qualities of your food and drinks about can either, among other things:

1. Cool down or warm up your body

2. Dry your system or provide adequate moisture

3. Energize your internal organs or draw energy out of your body

With a little preparation and processing, the intrinsic qualities of food determine the impact on our bodies.

One of the basic qualities of food is that it provides warmth when cooked, just like raw food is more likely to help the body cool down. That is why, during cold seasons such as winter, cooked foods are more appropriate because they provide much-needed body warmth. But when you eat more raw foods during the summer, this can help alleviate the impact of a hot and humid environment on your body.

It seems that these characteristics are ingrained in the human psyche. Even without reading this, it's natural for people to prefer soups and stews and other cooked foods when it's cold, and during hot and humid seasons like summer, many people prefer raw fruits and salads. Regardless of how instinctive or basic this seems, you'll be able to tap into your natural intuition more deeply and more accurately apply these principles with more skill when you take the time to understand them in more detail.

Your Food and the Environment

As mentioned earlier, seasons or weather have a say on what types of food are best for us at any given time. Similar to this, our surrounding environment also matters. It's because weather or seasons are largely dependent on your location. Living in a tropical country like the Philippines, where it's hot and humid most of the year, eating body-cooling foods is appropriate. In very cold places like Antarctica, cooked foods are the way to go.

The relationship between food and the environment is also evident in the types of foods available in certain areas of the world. Tropical fruits, for example, are more abundant in countries that lie near the equator. It isn't a coincidence that such foods are best for mitigating the effects of hot weather in tropical countries. This is one way that nature brings balance to the environment and the people who live in it.

When you eat in harmony with the environment in which you live, it'll be easier for you to get all the necessary nutrients for optimal health and wellbeing. One practical reason is that eating foods that naturally grow in your area maximizes your chances of obtaining and eating them fresh. Imported foods require long-haul transportation and possibly, either they're no longer as fresh or have been treated with preservatives. Neither of which leads to optimal health and wellbeing.

The Spiritual Component of Food

Particularly in western medicine, the primary belief is that food is purely physiological in nature. As such, it only looks at the physical impact or benefits of eating. Interestingly enough, a study showed the possibility that eating food may also have a spiritual or emotional aspect to it.

The study fed two groups of people the same meal, i.e., one loaded with cholesterol, sugar, salt, and saturated fats. The first group eats their meal in a noisy environment with lots of traffic and construction activities going on around them. The other group ate their meal in a relatively quiet place with gentle sounds and music playing in the background. Afterward, the researchers took the participants' blood pressures and triglyceride levels.

The findings were unexpected - at least for those who merely considered the physiological aspect of food. The food given to the participants was obviously harmful in terms of both blood pressure and triglyceride levels, but the results were different.

Both indicators rose in subjects who ate their meals in a very noisy environment. But both indicators for those who ate their meals in a relatively quiet environment went down. While this may not be very conclusive, it shows that the effects of food on the body may not necessarily depend completely on its physiological characteristics and nutrient profiles. A person's mental or emotional state, which may be influenced or affected by the eating environment, may also play a significant role.

Based on this study, there's more to our health and wellbeing than simply what we eat. It's highly possible that the way we interact with our food matters as well. To this extent, it is very important to have the right attitude when eating food. An attitude of gratitude may also be crucial to get the most benefits from the foods we eat.

Eating Properly for Adequate Qi

What are the best foods for optimal qi flow in your body? A generally healthy diet is naturally good for your qi. To optimize the latter, certain types of food are needed.

One guiding principle in choosing qi flow-optimizing food and drinks is the glycemic index, e.g., GI. This refers to the ability of the food you consume to raise blood sugar levels rapidly; specifically, the impact on the body's insulin response. All food and drinks lie within a spectrum between low glycemic index and high glycemic index.

The low glycemic index or low GI foods take time to break down in the stomach and be converted to glucose. As such, they don't immediately flood the bloodstream with glucose, and as a result, blood sugar levels remain relatively steady and minimize insulin production.

On the other end of the spectrum, high GI foods are those that are easily broken down and converted to glucose. As a result, glucose quickly enters the bloodstream and triggers greater insulin production.

Now, what's the deal about blood sugar levels and insulin production? When you eat a lot of foods high on the glycemic index, your blood sugar levels become very volatile. Then your blood sugar spikes and crashes which is its trademark.

Have you ever felt so energetic after downing a large serving of soda only to feel lethargic or even sleepy shortly thereafter? That happens when your blood sugar levels become volatile. When glucose quickly enters your bloodstream, it spikes up your blood sugar and makes you feel as if you have high energy. After your pancreas senses the sugar spike, it'll quickly produce lots of insulin to counteract it.

However, the problem with the pancreas is that it's not able to properly estimate the right amount of insulin needed to normalize blood sugar. As a result, it usually produces a lot of insulin to overcorrect your high blood sugar levels, dropping them below normal. Often called sugar crashes, this makes you feel lethargic or sleepy. When this happens, your body starts to intensely crave high GI foods again to bring blood sugar levels back to normal quickly. Then, the cycle continues. Blood sugar spikes again and crashes again, giving you that energetic then suddenly lethargic feeling all over again.

But when you eat mostly low glycemic index foods or carbohydrates, you enjoy the benefit of relatively steady blood sugar levels. This means they neither spike nor crash, which gives you a steady dose of energy throughout the day. This ability to consistently release energy into your system makes it an ideal food for the Qigong diet.

Some of the best sources of low GI or complex carbohydrates include whole-grain foods:

1. Barley

2. Brown rice

3. Buckwheat

4. Oatmeal

5. Quinoa

6. Sweet potatoes

7. Whole wheat bread

8. Foods made primarily of whole grain flour, such as pasta and noodles

Carbohydrates aren't necessarily one of two extremes, low and high GI. They may also lie between, i.e., mid glycemic index. If you have no choice but to eat mid or high GI carbohydrates, you can lower their glycemic index by eating them with protein and healthy dietary fats. This slows down their digestion and, ultimately, their conversion to glucose.

And speaking of proteins, the best ones for a Qigong-friendly diet are organic sources of white meat. Being organic, they don't contain GMO substances and/or steroids. White meat is preferred because, typically, they contain very little or no facts.

But of course, not everyone can afford organic food. That's why focusing mostly on white meat isn't just important but also practical. These include turkey or chicken breast.

Other excellent proteins and healthy dietary fat sources are seafood such as tuna, salmon, sardines, and cod. You may also get these from eggs, organic if possible. However, you must limit your weekly consumption of these foods.

Some excellent protein sources include tofu, legumes, rice milk, soya milk, and soy yogurt to go vegetarian or vegan.

Consistent with traditional Chinese medicine principles, a healthy, Qigong-friendly diet includes a lot of vegetables. If you can afford to, go for organic and locally grown ones. They're both pesticide-free and are as fresh as possible. The best way to eat them is raw. If you prefer to eat them cooked, steaming or stir-frying them is ideal. Other excellent plant sources of key nutrients include seeds, nuts, beans, and soya bean curd or tofu.

Two other excellent plant foods to include in a Qigong-based diet are kelp and nori. Both are made from seaweed and contain lots of phytonutrients, especially antioxidants.

Last, try not to microwave your food or, at the very least, limit them. Doing this depletes your foods available qi.

For a Qigong-based diet, there are two main types of foods you need to include as much as possible: qi-building and deficiency-reducing. Some of the best qi-building foods include:

1. Almonds

2. Apples

3. Asparagus

4. Barley

5. Beef

6. Berries

7. Black sesame seeds

8. Buckwheat

9. Button mushrooms

10. Cabbages

11. Cheese

12. cherries

13. Chicken (especially breast)

14. Chicken liver

15. Coconuts

16. Corn

17. Dates

18. Duck

19. Eel

20. Eggplants

21. Figs

22. Goose

23. Ham

24. Herring

25. Honey

26. Lamb

27. Lentils

28. Logans

29. Mackerel

30. Malt

31. Milk

32. Mussels

33. Oats

34. Octopi

35. Oysters

36. Peanuts

37. Potatoes

38. Rice syrup

39. Rice

40. Squash

41. Sweet potatoes

42. Tomatoes

43. Trout

44. Tunas

45. Turkey (especially breast)

46. Walnuts

47. Wheat bran

48. Yam

49. Yogurt

50. Supplements such as pollen, royal jelly, algae, and ginseng

Excellent foods for rectifying qi deficiencies include:

1. Apples

2. Beef

3. Cherries

4. Chicken

5. Dates

6. Figs

7. Goose meat

8. Ham

9. Lamb

10. Licorice

11. Loganberries

12. Molasses

13. Oats

14. Rice

15. Squash

16. Sweet potatoes

17. Sweet rice

18. Tofu

19. Yams

20. Supplements like pollen, algae, royal jelly, and American ginseng

And to ensure optimal qi through your diet, avoid or minimize these types of foods:

1. Artificial flavorings

2. Food coloring

3. High-glycemic index carbs (sugar-loaded foods) like soda, juices, raw sugars, candies, cakes, etc.

4. Refined, processed, and/or canned foods

5. Synthetic preservatives

6. White bread

7. White flour

8. White rice

Chapter 10: A Daily Qigong Routine

For your daily practice, it's important to remember that Qigong isn't just a physical practice but a mental one as well. Every Qigong session involves the following physical and mental aspects:

1. Calming down the mind and focusing your intention

2. Right postures that facilitate the free flow of your energy

3. Controlling your breath to stimulate your qi and body

4. Being aware of your energy or qi

Before anything else, let's talk about awareness levels first. You see, qigong exercises provide benefits on different levels. These include:

1. Stretching, working, and loosening joints and muscles in your body

2. Coordination of your movements with your breath

3. Creation and storage of qi or energy in the Dantian, which helps you learn to balance the body relative to forces of the exercises' movements and gravity

4. Giving your internal organs and their connecting nerves a healthy massage

5. Stimulation of energy flow through your medians related to the organs

Because of these, being aware of your energy or qi involves different levels, which include:

1. Awareness of the sensations in your spine, joints, and muscles while performing the movements

2. Awareness of each breath's stretching and releasing effects on your movements

3. Awareness of your Dantian

4. Awareness of the internal massage for your organs

5. Awareness of how your qi or energy is flowing with your meridian

To develop awareness, learn just a few exercises at a time. When you are comfortable and aware of how each movement feels, start adding one or two exercises to your daily sessions. Continue adding the others until you can practice them all comfortably. You must know completely how the movements feel in your spine, joints, and muscles.

Once you've developed an awareness of the sensations of the movements, it's time to work on becoming aware of your breathing and, more importantly, its stretching and releasing effects during your exercise movements. One way to do this is by coordinating your breath with the movements. For example, exhale when the movement involves moving your limbs away from your body and inhaling as you move them back towards it.

Once you have become aware of your breath and how it impacts your movements, the next level is awareness of your Dantian. In particular, it's about being mindful of how your body expands and contracts around it.

Next, it's time to work on developing awareness of specific organs and being internally massaged during your exercise sessions. Your ability to do this can help you learn how to perform the Qigong exercises in the right sequence based on the time of the day.

Last, you also need to be aware of how your qi or energy flows along specific meridians. This can be challenging at first because awareness can be quite subtle. Over time and with constant practice, you'll be able to feel it more and more.

Remember that developing all levels of awareness is more of a marathon than a race or a sprint. Take your time developing each awareness level one at a time, and by doing this, instead of jumping the learning curve by working on all levels simultaneously, you'll be able to establish a solid foundation for your daily Qigong exercise routines.

Remember that the exercises need to be performed with minimum muscular tension (positions that are as relaxed as possible) and in slow, flowing movements. The slower your movements, the more beneficial they can be.

However, it's also important to remember that your Qigong practice shouldn't feel strained or uncomfortable. Hence, go as slow as comfortably possible. When it becomes uncomfortable, you're probably doing it too slow and, thus, may need to increase the speed slightly.

Initially, don't worry if you're unable to move as slow as seasoned practitioners. As a beginner, it's normal. Gradually slow down your movements during several days, weeks, or even months as you regularly perform them. Eventually, you'll be able to develop the necessary fitness and stamina to go as slow as possible and maximize the benefits of regular Qigong exercise.

Again, don't rush your movements to complete the required number of repetitions of your exercises quickly. If you're pressed for time, prioritize comfort over the need to finish your target repetitions at all costs. The key is to perform the movements in a relaxed and flowing manner. When you force yourself to finish a specific number of reps within a limited amount of time, you may end up performing them improperly, rushing the movements, and forfeiting much of the exercises' benefits.

Before we go to the exercises themselves, you must know that if your personal circumstances or physical condition makes standing exercises very difficult or impossible, you may perform them sitting down with minor modifications to the movements. The ideal sitting position is one where you're on the edge of a bench, chair, or stool and at a height that allows your thighs/hamstrings to be as parallel as possible to the floor. Sitting this way helps you ensure proper posture for your spine during the exercises.

Sitting this way also helps you learn to assume the horse stance or ma bu excellently. It also helps maximize the stretching effect on your spine, which, in turn, can help you improve flexibility in your lower back muscles. Eventually, it can make assuming the standing horse stance with your pelvis tucked under much easier.

Awareness of Energy

The most important benefit associated with Qigong exercises is optimal development and circulation of the qi or energy throughout your body. The earlier you recognize and actually feel this energy, the quicker your progress can be.

When trying to become aware of your qi, you'll experience several sensations. One of the most common feelings is that of two opposite poles of a magnet being drawn together or being pushed apart. Another one is a warm fuzzy feeling. Others note, feeling it tinkling or breeze-like sensation on their skin. As you continue with your Qigong journey, you will likely experience these sensations and probably more.

It's possible that from the get-go, you may already start to feel them. It may also take you some time. Regardless, the important thing is to acknowledge those sensations as they come. Neither force nor convince yourself to feel sensations that aren't really there. Just be consistent in practicing these exercises, and in time, you become aware of your qi.

The moment you become aware of feeling your energy, you can develop it regardless of how subtle it is. Over time and with regular practice, you learn to use your mind to direct your qi to the specific areas of your body and, eventually, increase your recognition and sensitivity to them.

At first, you'll likely be most aware of the qi in your hands. Why? It's because it's one of the body parts that you tend to be most aware of, considering how frequently you use them to hold, feel, and use things. Also, there are a lot of nerve endings in your hands, and blood flows to them easily compared to other body parts.

With continuous practice, you'll feel the energy start to develop in your arms and ultimately develop in your legs until you feel it all over your body.

A very practical way to start developing awareness of your energy is by doing this simple exercise:

> 1. Clap your hands robustly and intermittently for at least one minute. You should feel a warm and possibly tingling sensation in your hands by the time you stop clapping. This is a positive sign because all that clapping helps stimulate the nerve endings in your hands, resulting in increased blood flow in said area. Remember, qi flow is closely linked to blood flow and nervous system functioning; hence the tingling sensation makes you aware of your energy.

2. Now, join your hands in front of you but just short of touching. As you do this and hold the position, you'll be able to feel a warm sensation between your hands because of all that clapping.

3. Next, start moving your hands in and out slightly first by bringing them close together (not touching) then pulling them far apart enough you can still feel the warmth between your hands.

4. As you continue doing this, gradually increase the distance between your hands. Over time and with enough practice, you'll start feeling something similar to a magnetic push or pull between your hands while moving them.

5. While increasing the distance between your hands when pulling them apart, imagine a warm sphere of magnetic energy pushing back against your hands and growing. As you bring them closer together, think about squeezing that ball.

6. Always remember to breathe.

While many people can start feeling their qi the first time they do this exercise, others don't. If you're one of the latter, don't worry. With consistent practice, you should be able to feel it, too. Coupling this exercise, together with the other ones in this chapter, helps increase your awareness and your ability to control your qi.

Here are some exercises to help increase your awareness of your qi.

String Pulling

1. Begin by standing with a relaxed posture.

2. In your mind's eye, see a ring between your feet just in front of you.

3. Visualize a piece of string passing through the said ring, with one end tied to your left middle finger and the other two you're right middle finger.

4. As you start lifting your right hand. As you do, move your left hand down towards the direction of the imaginary ring. It should feel as though the ring is some kind of pulley through which your imaginary string passes through in that as you pull one hand up, it pulls the other one down towards the ring.

5. Pull your left hand upward and in the process, imagine that the string attached to your left middle finger is pulling your right hand down towards the ring.

6. Feel the pull of the string in one hand on the other as you alternately lift each hand.

Another way to perform this exercise is by replacing the imaginary string with an imaginary energy column instead. One end of this column is attached to your left hand and the other to your right hand. Like the imaginary string, imagine passing through a fixed point on the floor between your feet. As with the string, imagine one hand being pulled down as the other is raised alternately.

Wall Pushes

1. Begin by standing straight and close to a wall.

2. Raise both hands in front of you such that your arms are perpendicular to your torso.

3. Move your hands very close to the wall, but not touching it, before moving them away from it.

4. Every time you bring your hands very close to the wall, feel the energy between them being compressed. Doing this helps you feel a magnetic force pushing back against your hands as you compress them against the wall.

The Energy Ball

1. Begin by moving your hands close together until you start to feel an energy ball between them.

2. Next, start moving your hands in a round motion just like you would when rubbing around a basketball, a soccer ball, or any kind of ball.

3. As you continue moving your hands in a circular motion, gradually increase the distance between them while continuing to feel the sensation of rubbing the energy ball's surface.

4. Wait for your energy ball to expand to your desired size. At this point, start squeezing it while continuing the circular motion of your hands. Doing this may make you feel the energy ball heating up and warming your hands. You may also feel an increasing magnetic feel and the ball becoming heavier.

An Overview of Your Qigong Sessions

Each Qigong session comprises three important aspects: the warm-up, the exercises, and the cool-down. You can refer to chapter 7 for the warm-up exercises.

For the exercise proper itself, you must perform them in order based on what time of the day you're practicing. You may begin with ones linked to organs whose peak activities coincide with the time of the day you're doing Qigong exercises. Then, perform the other exercises according to their peak activity time, ending your sessions back with exercises linked to the organ that's currently at peak activity.

Pay close attention to how you feel and your breathing throughout your Qigong sessions. Should you feel dizzy, short of breath, or very uncomfortable at any point, stop for a while and take a break. Let a minute or two passed by so your energy and breathing normalize before resuming your session.

At the end of your workout, start the cool-down process. Place both hands on the base of your abdomen, just in front of your Dantian. Feel the energy in it and pay close attention to your breathing, which must be slow and steady.

Continue cooling down by massaging different parts of your body related to your meridians' energy flow directions. Do this by patting, rubbing, or running your hands along the surface of your body. Do this towards the direction of your meridians but without touching it. By doing this, you can facilitate energy distribution all over your body to help you feel refreshed and stimulated.

You can cap off the cool-down process by putting your hands back on top of your lower abs. As you do this, become aware of your Dantian and your breathing again for a few minutes.

As you end your Qigong routine, it's important to properly cool down as with any form of exercise. Here are some exercises for ending your sessions properly.

The Energy Massage

1. Start by standing street with feet about shoulder-width apart and both hands resting on your lower belly. While in this position, take your time and be aware of your breath and your Dantian.

2. Next, pull your hands apart and place them on your lower back. Gradually, run them down the sides of your lower body, starting from the lower back to your hips, calves, and feet.

3. Place your hands on the insides of your feet. Move them up the inside of your calves and thighs. Then, put your hands in front of your stomach and run them upward to your chest.

4. Extend your left arm to the side, then run your right hand along its inside, starting from the shoulder all the way to the left hand.

5. Next, turn your left arm over and run back your right hand along the outside of the arm, passing over the elbow, until it returns back to your right chest.

6. Bring your left hand back to your left chest and extend the right hand to the side.

7. Run your left hand along the inside of your right arm, starting from the shoulder all the way to the hand.

8. Turn over your right arm and run your left hand back along the outside of the arm until it goes back to the left chest.

9. With both hands now in front of your chest, run them both along your face and up your head. Continue running them down your nape, shoulders, and behind your waist.

10. This constitutes one repetition. You may repeat this as often as you want.

11. To end this massage, bring both hands back to your lower stomach. Bring your focus back to your breathing and your Dantian.

Benefit Specific Qigong Routines

The routines above help you experience the many health and wellbeing benefits of Qigong. If you want shorter sessions that focus on specific benefits, here are some daily routines you can try.

Vitality Routine

This one helps stimulate most of your acupuncture meridians and internal organs and invigorate your body. Here's how to do it:

1. Start by assuming a comfortable, grounded standing position, with feet about shoulder-width or slightly wider than shoulder-width apart. Let your arms hang on the sides.

2. Take a few deep breaths, inhaling through the nose and exhaling through the mouth. Be aware of your breathing.

3. Start the routine by bringing your arms sideward-up over your head in an elliptical manner. Inhale deeply while doing this.

4. Bring your hands down the front-middle of your body. Lower your body by squatting slightly until your hands are in front of your thighs. Exhale as you do this.

5. Raise your hands and arms in an elliptical motion. Stop when both of your hands are at the top of your head. Inhale as you do this.

6. Repeat the last two steps 5-6 times.

7. Assume the starting position with feet about shoulder-width apart or slightly wider, with arms relaxed on your side.

8. Keeping your arms limp, swing them like pendulums from side to side by moving your weight sideways. It's like performing multiple golf swings in opposite directions in successive fashion, but with limp arms. Perform this movement 10 to 20 times.

9. Next, raise your arms and hands in front of your body up to chest level, with palms facing each other while you inhale. Keeping arms extended, move them as far back as possible without discomfort to open your torso/chest. Continue inhaling.

10. Close your chest by moving your arms forward until your hands are in front of your middle chest but not touching each other while exhaling. With palms facing down, bring your arms down while squatting slightly until your hands are at mid-thigh level. Continue exhaling at this point.

11. Repeat steps 9 and 10 ten times.

12. Go back to the starting position, but with a wider than shoulder-width stance and toes pointed outward at roughly 45 degrees.

13. Breathe in while bringing your extended arms up – palms facing the sky – in front of your body while breathing in. Once your hands are at eye level, turn your palms over and bring the arms down until the hands are at waist level while squatting and exhaling. The lowest you should squat is the point where your knees are in a vertical line with your toes or when it starts to feel too strenuous, whichever comes first.

14. Turn your palms up and raise your arms until the hands are at eye level while standing back up and inhaling deeply.

15. Repeat steps 13 and 14 ten times.

16. Go back to the starting position.

17. Bring your palms in front of your belly, facing up. Breathe in deeply while bringing them up to chest level.

18. Turn your palms over and push them down up to the crotch area while exhaling.

19. Repeat steps 17 & 18 ten times.

20. Go back to the starting position and take several deep breaths to end.

Stress Relief, Energy, and Vitality Routine

1. Start by assuming a comfortable, grounded standing position, with feet about shoulder-width or slightly wider than shoulder-width apart. Let your arms hang on the sides.

2. Take a few deep breaths, inhaling through the nose and exhaling through the mouth. Be aware of your breathing.

3. Start the routine by bringing your arms sideward-up over your head in an elliptical manner. Inhale deeply while doing these.

4. Bring your hands down the middle-front of your body with palms facing down. Lower your body slightly squatting until your hands are in front of your thighs. Exhale as you do this.

5. Raise your hands and arms in an elliptical motion. Stop at the top of your head. Inhale as you do these.

6. Repeat the last two steps 5-6 times.

7. Assume the starting position.

8. Breathe in as you bring your hands up the middle-front of your body. Stop when they're above your head.

9. Bring your hands down in an elliptical motion while exhaling. Simultaneously, squat slightly until your hands are in front of your thighs. They should be slightly below crotch level.

10. While inhaling and standing back up, raise your hands back up along the center of your body.

11. Repeat steps 8 to 10 ten times.

12. Go back to the starting position, but with a slightly wider than shoulder-width stance this time. Extend your right hand to your side and make a big circle with it in front of your body. Your palms should face the direction of the movement.

13. During the downward phase of the circle, slightly lunge toward the movement. During the sideward movement at the bottom portion of the circle, shift your lunge to the other side. Stand back up during the upward phase of the motion.

14. Repeat steps 12 to 13 ten times before doing another ten repetitions with the other hand.

15. Go back to the starting position with a normal, shoulder-width stance.

16. Turn to the right side with your right foot forward and the left one planted at a 45-degree angle at the back. Your hips must face the right side.

17. Extend your arms in front of your chest, palms closely facing each other and fingers pointing forward.

18. Breathe in as you draw your palms to your chest and fingers pointing upwards, e.g., praying hands. As you do this, move backward by shifting your body weight to your hind leg, i.e., the left one. Keep both feet planted on the ground.

19. With palms still facing each other, draw the largest circle you can with them. As you bring them down along the center of your body and raising them as far forward as you can up to chest level, breathe out. Shift your body weight forward to your right leg as you do this.

20. As you draw your palms towards your chest, shift your weight backward to your left leg and breathe in.

21. Repeat steps 17 to 20 ten times before doing the same with the left leg in front and the right one behind.

22. Go back to the starting position, with feet shoulder-width apart.

23. Start by shifting your weight to the left side of your body, with your right hand raised to the left side of your face, about 6 inches away. Put your left hand down your left side.

24. Shift your body weight to the right in a sliding manner, with your right leg now supporting it. Keep both feet planted on the ground. As you do, slide your left hand to the front of your right hip and reposition your right hand to the left side of your face, the palm facing it. Inhale while doing this.

25. Switch hand positions, i.e., bring your left hand up to the right side of your face and your right hand down on the right side of your body. Shift your body weight in a sliding motion back to the left, sliding your right hand to the front of your left hip, and repositioning your left hand to the left side of your face. Exhale while doing this.

26. Repeat steps 23-25 ten to twenty times.

27. Assume the starting position but with arms as if you're hugging a tree. Keep fingers an inch apart, and your knees slightly bent. Breathe deeply and naturally while drawing qi from the earth. Keep your body relaxed with as little tension as possible to keep your arms up as long as possible. Hold the position for as long as comfortably possible.

Tips to Maximize Your Qigong Routine Benefits

To enjoy the benefits of Qigong practice, consistency is of utmost importance. If you want to maximize them, you can supplement them with other practices. The following are some ways to do this.

Preparation

As cliche as it sounds, "failing to plan is planning to fail" has a great deal of truth to it. As another saying goes, what gets scheduled gets done.

Adequate preparation involves blocking off time for your regular Qigong practice. It doesn't just happen; naturally, you have to make time for it. If you're a morning person, considering sleeping early so you can wake up earlier and make time for Qigong. Or if you're more of an evening person, try to end your day earlier so you'll have enough time to do it at night just before you go to bed. If you're neither, consider using your lunch break to do this in a quiet and private area at work.

Another aspect of preparation is energy management. This means eating healthy foods in the right amounts and getting enough sleep. As you learned earlier in the chapter on the Qigong diet, eat lower GI, complex carbs, lean protein, and healthy fats. Doing so will help you enjoy steady energy throughout the day so you can consistently practice Qigong on top of your other daily duties.

There is no specific benchmark for how many hours you need every night for sleep because each person is different. On average, you may need anywhere between seven to nine hours of sleep at night for optimal energy throughout the day. The best way you can estimate your nightly sleep requirements yes by sleeping at the same time at night and not waking up with an alarm. Start a sleeping journal, and on it, take note of how many hours of sleep you got the previous night, and more importantly, how you felt the next day. After about a week or two of sleep journaling, you'll be able to get an idea of your personal sleep requirements.

Another way to sleep optimally is by adjusting your sleeping or waking hours according to the average sleep cycle, which is about 90 minutes or 1-1/2 hours. Using this cycle, you can either determine what time to sleep based on your wake-up time or adjust the latter based on the time you want to sleep at night. A very useful app for this is sleep time, which is an android app. If your wake-up time is non-negotiable, you can type it in the app, and it will tell you what hours are best for you to hit the sack. If you have more leeway in terms of waking up in the morning, you can type in the time you want to sleep, and it will show you the best times to wake up per the 90-minute sleep cycle.

Patience

We live in a world that seeks to get results as fast as possible, hence the reference to a microwave society. However, the best things in life often take time to accomplish or experience. The awesome health and wellbeing benefits of Qigong are among those.

Instead of focusing on the benefits themselves, make developing Qigong into a habit your primary goal. By doing so, you'll be less pressured to reap the benefits quickly, and chances are, it will be easier for you to slow down and enjoy the practice itself. If you successfully develop this habit, regular practice will no longer be a struggle, and the benefits will automatically and consistently come.

But if you hurry things up, you're increasing the likelihood of being unable to experience Qigong's benefits. For one, trying to speed up the process can lead to overexertion. In turn, this can lead to burnout, injuries, or worse, both.

Remember, Rome wasn't built in a day, but they were busy laying bricks by the hour. Experiencing optimal health and wellbeing through Qigong takes time, but it'll be worth the wait.

Find Your Why

Last, you must have a compelling reason for engaging in Qigong and making it a regular part of your life. Without one, you'll likely give up once things become inconvenient or even hard. If you have a very compelling reason for wanting to practice it, you'll find enough strength and fortitude to continue even when the going gets rough.

While it's good to pursue Qigong for optimal health and wellbeing, I don't think it's compelling enough for most people. Why? It's a very general or vague motivation. It's not personal enough. A more compelling reason related to health and wellbeing could be not wanting to be a burden to the family because of sickness and disease. Another one is enjoying as many years as possible with your spouse. In other words, your reasons for engaging in the practice should be something very personal and can be achieved with optimal health and well-being.

Qigong Exercises

Qi Locks

These are hand positions required in some of the Qigong exercises. They're meant to help keep your qi or energy flowing within your body and prevent it from leaking out.

The first qi lock resembles a fist, only that the thumb is inside the four fingers instead of covering them. This is a very useful type of qi lock because many of your meridians end with the fingertips. Since this position brings all the fingers of your hand inward to your palm, it allows you to build up qi and keep it flowing inside your body.

Another qi lock used in the exercises is called the crane's head. You lock your hands by bringing all five fingertips of your hand together. This helps facilitate optimal qi circulation and keeps it from leaking.

Conclusion

Qigong is one of the best investments you can make that can help you live an optimally healthy, joy-filled, and satisfying life. Practicing it daily doesn't cost a penny. It's not as strenuous as most other forms of exercise, and most importantly, its benefits can be truly life-changing. Now that you have read this book, you are in a great position to start practicing it and be on your way to an optimally healthy and vigorous life.

However, the knowledge you've gained here is just potential power. To unleash its true power, you must practice what you've learned as soon as possible. The longer you procrastinate, the higher your risks of not doing the practice and, ultimately, missing out on the kind of life it can give.

Hence, practice what you've learned immediately. Remember, you don't have to practice everything all at once. Just start with one or two exercises and take baby steps first. That way, you already start moving the needle at a pace that will not lead to burnout. Baby steps are more likely to be consistent, and Qigong's benefits require consistency. So, better to start taking small steps now than none at all.

Here's to your health and wellbeing, my friend!

Here's another book by Mari Silva that you might like

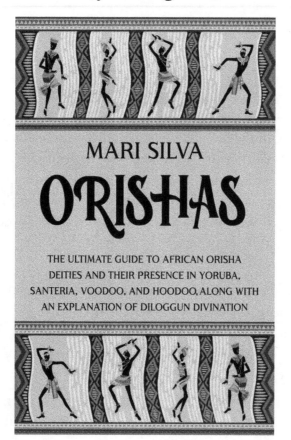

Three Intentful Corrections & Principles of Movement – Supercharge Your Life! www.relaxedandalert.com/teacher-training-library/lecture/three-intentful-corrections-principles-of-movement-2.

"Welcome to Taiji Forum - a Universe of Chinese Arts." Taiji Forum, taiji-forum.com/.

"What Are the Health Benefits of Qigong?" Health Essentials from Cleveland Clinic, 23 Sept. 2020,

health.clevelandclinic.org/what-are-the-health-benefits-of-Qigong/.